D0921398

SINCE 1939

BALLET · FILMS

MUSIC · PAINTING

'THE ARTS IN BRITAIN' SERIES

A series of booklets by writers of authority in their own respective spheres; fully illustrated, in some cases in colour

ARCHITECTURE IN ENGLAND *by John Summerson*

BALLET SINCE 1939 *by Arnold L. Haskell*

DRAMA SINCE 1939 *by Robert Speaight*

FILMS SINCE 1939 *by Dilys Powell*

MUSIC SINCE 1939 *by Rollo Myers*

THE NOVEL SINCE 1939 *by Henry Reed*

PAINTING SINCE 1939 *by Robin Ironside*

POETRY SINCE 1939 *by Stephen Spender*

PROSE LITERATURE SINCE 1939 *by John Hayward*

SCOTTISH ART *by Ian Finlay*

THE VOICE OF WALES *by Wyn Griffith*

Published by Longmans Green & Co. Ltd.
for the British Council

Spectre de la Rose—Drop Curtain by Rex Whistler

SINCE 1939

BALLET · FILMS

MUSIC · PAINTING

by

Arnold L. Haskell
Dilys Powell
Rollo Myers
Robin Ironside

One hundred illustrations in colour and monochrome

LONDON · PHOENIX HOUSE
by arrangement with the British Council

730

This book is copyright. It may not be reproduced whole or in part by any method without written permission. Application should be made in the first place to Phoenix House

Made 1948 in Great Britain. Set and printed at Edinburgh by R. & R. Clark Ltd., for

PHOENIX HOUSE LIMITED

38 William IV Street, London

First published in book form 1948. The four titles were originally issued as separate brochures in 1946/7 by Longmans Green & Co. Ltd. for the British Council

This book is produced in complete conformity with the authorised economy standards

CONTENTS

UNIFORM WITH THIS VOLUME

SINCE 1939

THE NOVEL · PROSE LITERATURE
POETRY · DRAMA

by

Henry Reed
John Hayward
Stephen Spender
Robert Speaight

PHOENIX HOUSE

ILLUSTRATIONS

BALLET SINCE 1939

TO

J. D. NEWTH

SOUVENIR OF A LONG AND
HAPPY ASSOCIATION

A. L. H.

ARNOLD L. HASKELL

BALLET SINCE 1939

NO WRITER in this country has been more active in promoting the cause of British Ballet than has Mr. Arnold Haskell. After the death of Diaghileff in 1929, at a time when it seemed possible that interest in the ballet in this country would not survive his inspiring genius, Arnold Haskell was one of a small group of enthusiasts who kept the ballet alive until, with the emergence of Sadler's Wells, we had for the first time the basis of a National Ballet.

Mr. Haskell has already published a number of books on various aspects of the ballet, including *Some Studies in Ballet*, *Balletomania*, *Diaghileff*, *Prelude to Ballet*, *Ballet Panorama*, *The National Ballet*, etc. In the present essay he sets out for the first time the story of British ballet during the years of war, years during which the art of the ballet caught more strongly than ever the imagination of the British public.

CONTENTS

ILLUSTRATIONS

BALLET SINCE 1939

I. THE BIRTH OF BRITISH BALLET

1. *Introduction*

In the early seventeenth century a foreign visitor to this country remarked that the English excelled in dancing and making music. I believe that to be a true characteristic, hidden for a time by the accidents of history but always there, ready to emerge at a suitable opportunity. England's folk-dances and village festivals, as distinct from those in Scotland, where the tradition is strong, may largely have disappeared, to be resurrected this century with scholarship and difficulty by the admirable English Folk Dance Society—early English music has already inspired one great composer, Vaughan Williams,—but the desire and the ability to dance have always been present. In Jacobean and Caroline times they revealed themselves in the Masque, an English art form that called upon poet, composer, singer, dancer and architect, and that survives today only in the words of Milton's *Comus*, the cartoons of Inigo Jones and the scores of Purcell, Arne and others. But in recent times they have revealed themselves most strongly in the Western European theatrical form of ballet, an art born at the court of King Louis XIV, that was fostered by Molière, Lully, Rameau, Noverre and others, finding the high approbation of Voltaire, that travelled through Italy where it was developed technically and systematised by Carlo Blasis and that finally found its most complete form of expression in Russia. When the extremes of romanticism had made the art sterile elsewhere, driving it to the music-hall in England, Russian artists were developing it as an artistic medium. Our British ballet today is directly inspired by the example and practice of the Russian ballet, exported to Western Europe by Serge Diaghileff and his group of artists, and is in the direct line of tradition that can easily be traced from the source.[1] Tradition is all-important in an art form that leaves no exact written record.

[1] See the Appendix, p. 51.

London had always produced enthusiastic audiences for ballet. In the glorious days of Taglioni, Grisi, Grahn and Cerrito, Théophile Gautier writes of the tremendous enthusiasm of the London audience but doubts its critical faculties. Over half a century later, when ballet, with the glorious exception of a Genée, had reached its lowest ebb and was rescued by Pavlova and more especially Diaghileff, it was in London that these artists found their largest audiences and their biggest financial backing. The history of British ballet is prefaced by the history of ballet in Britain.

2. *Russian Ballet in England*

It is with Pavlova and Diaghileff that the story of British ballet began.

Pavlova, in difficulties with the temperamental clashes between the Russian and Polish members of her company, found the British dancer as quick to learn and far more amenable to discipline. Soon her company was filled with English girls. This, whatever her motive, was of first-class importance. Previously the English dancer could find an outlet only in the music-hall or yearly pantomime. Pavlova gave the profession an artistic status that encouraged girls to learn and that reassured the parents of the stage-struck. Ballet was now judged to be no less respectable than piano or violin. It is obvious that in the Pavlova company Pavlova alone counted, but her action gave a generation of English girls the opportunity not only to learn but to prove to themselves and to the public that they could dance.

With Diaghileff it was a different matter. For a long time his company was in fact the travelling branch of the Russian Imperial Theatres, and even after the connection was severed he relied on Russia for his dancers. Only one English girl distinguished herself in the early days (1912). Her name was Hilda Munnings, but it is significant that her great career was made as Lydia Sokolova and that until 1918 few people penetrated her disguise. After the revolution Diaghileff's supply of dancers from his mother-country failed and he turned to Britain to find such brilliant artists as Vera Savina, Ninette de Valois, Alicia Markova and Anton Dolin.

In spite of these disguises their nationality became known and to Diaghileff's annoyance their number was greatly exaggerated in the press. But those Muscovite names were justified; artistically they were Russians, trained in the Russian school, living as part of a Russian tradition. The time for a British national ballet had not yet come, though its dancers were receiving their education. And Diaghileff himself clearly foresaw the birth of an indigenous British ballet. It could only come to pass after his death; he did not tolerate rivals, however humble.

The death of Diaghileff (1929) released a number of highly trained dancers, trained not only technically but artistically. There were also countless dancers in the schools all over Britain, whose one ambition was to dance in his ranks. Were they all to be disappointed? Was ballet to find its way back to the music-hall, sandwiched in between the juggler and the performing seal?

3. *The Camargo Society*

Before this could happen a group of dancers and artists, invited to meet by P. J. S. Richardson, editor of *The Dancing Times*, and Arnold L. Haskell, formed the Camargo Society, for the giving of ballet performances to subscription audiences four times a year. Edwin Evans, President of the Society for Contemporary Music, was Chairman. Working under great difficulties, this society formed a shop window for the remarkable talent left stranded by the death of Diaghileff: both the members of his company and those who might have joined it one day.

The Camargo was a management without a permanent company, a society only able to help those already making some effort to help themselves. It was magnificently successful and was able to wind up after two years when it had fulfilled its purpose and could hand over the task to a permanent body. During its short existence it developed two major choreographers in Ninette de Valois and Frederick Ashton, and produced *Job* (Vaughan Williams), *Pomona* and *Rio Grande* (Constant Lambert) and *Façade* (William Walton), the first all-British works. But it must be made clear that the policy of the society was never a chauvinistic one; its aim was to present the best within its means. From its birth, British ballet has produced an equal number of works of foreign origin, following in this respect the example of Russian ballet, which, wisely, was never deliberately national in outlook. Ballet can never be rigidly exclusive. The dance had enriched itself by drawing on the culture of the whole world and can only live while it continues to do so.

The Camargo Society depended in the main on two studio groups for its company, though such great artists as Lydia Lopokova, Phyllis Bedells, Alicia Markova and Anton Dolin gave their services. The first group was that of Marie Rambert, the second that of Ninette de Valois.

4. *Marie Rambert and the Ballet Club*

Marie Rambert, a pupil of Jaques-Dalcroze, first came to the Russian Ballet to teach Nijinsky eurhythmics. She remained to learn the classical ballet technique from Cecchetti. A wide experience and the nature of an enthusiast—she has always believed in the ugly duckling—soon made her London studio a laboratory of talent. At the time of Diaghileff's death she had a group consisting of Pearl Argyle, Andrée Howard, Diana Gould, Prudence Hyman, William Chappell, Frederick Ashton and many others, all of whom play a large role in our story. (Chappell's works have been few since 1939. He volunteered for military service at the outbreak of war.) This group she kept intact and formed into a small company that gave seasons at the Lyric, Hammersmith, and later at her own Mercury Theatre, headquarters of her Ballet Club. Her performances differed greatly from the average pupil show. Her dancers were young but never amateurish and they had a quality never before associated with the English dancer, personality. With Pavlova it had been discouraged, with Diaghileff disguised. Rambert exploited it, launching Ashton and others as choreographers, Chappell as a scenic artist and the beautiful Pearl Argyle as ballerina, the first to shine under a British name. In spite of her own undertakings, of which more will be said later, Marie Rambert threw herself whole-heartedly into the work of the Camargo.

5. *Ninette de Valois and Sadler's Wells*

The other studio group composing the Camargo Society was that of Ninette de Valois.

Ninette de Valois, *née* Edris Stannus, was a young Irish dancer, who miraculously survived being called a "child genius" to join the Diaghileff Ballet in 1923. She rapidly came to the fore as a *soliste*, but unlike any ordinary dancer she had other ambitions. She was daring enough to doubt the line that Diaghileff was taking, conduct that savoured of *lèse-majesté*. She left when almost at the top of the dancing ladder to produce plays for two famous *avant-garde* theatres, the Abbey, Dublin, and The Festival, Cambridge. And as if the journey between England and Ireland were not enough she formed her own choreographic group. Her work was known to few and showed no spectacular sign of promise. She seemed to be losing her way, a grimly earnest young rebel groping with singular intensity for some new form of dance-drama.

De Valois' fame was made in one night and it laid the foundations of a national ballet under her guidance.

The work presented by the Camargo Society that night in 1931 was *Job*, a danced interpretation of the Bible story as seen through the eyes of the poet-painter Blake, to a noble score by Vaughan Williams; a truly British inspiration. The work was immediately acclaimed; perhaps a little grudgingly in some quarters. Critics do not like to be caught out. This ballet was followed by Milhaud's *Création du Monde*, another heroic subject treated in the grand manner.

These successes led to an arrangement with Lilian Baylis, that remarkable woman who had brought Shakespeare and opera to the masses at her famous theatre, the "Old Vic", in the Waterloo Road. She had just acquired a second theatre, Sadler's Wells, in an equally populous and unfashionable district and wanted a permanent ballet for her opera. Lilian Baylis' motto was, "If you want anything done, always go to the very best person. The best people understand." Since she was always in debt she added, "and they are usually prepared to do the work for its own sake". They were, *for her*, and the greatest names in the theatre were proud to work at the " Vic " for a pittance. Single-handed she founded a true people's theatre movement.

There are many anecdotes told about her; she has become a legendary figure. One in particular, a true story, shows something of her courage and single-mindedness. She had just bought Sadler's Wells and was motoring to a rendezvous when she met with an accident. A policeman picked her up: " Why, it's Lilian Baylis of the Old Vic! "—" And Sadler's Wells," she had time to murmur before falling into a faint.

Her proposal to gather a few girls together to dance in the opera ballets cannot have seemed very tempting to the creator of *Job* who was now receiving lucrative offers from the commercial theatre. The ballet in *Faust* or *Carmen* is usually regarded as a sop to the tired business man, and its creator is anonymous in spite of the customary programme acknowledgment. But with Lilian Baylis' offer went the creation of a ballet school attached to the theatre, and de Valois realised where this could lead. Within a short time the Sadler's Wells Ballet [1] was firmly established, a rival to the opera company it had been created to serve. Lilian Baylis had made a new gift to Britain.

Both the Camargo Society, its offspring the Sadler's Wells Ballet and, to a lesser degree, Ballet Rambert were assisted by the " Anglo-Russians ". Alicia Markova starred with all three and brought the great theatre public with her. Anton Dolin appeared as guest artist, as did also the great Russian ballerina, Lydia Lopokova, who acted as godparent to the English venture, while her late husband, then Mr. J. M. Keynes (afterwards Lord Keynes, no less well known as a patron of the arts and the President of the Arts Council than as England's leading economist), wisely guided its financial policy as well as giving it artistic assistance.

English ballet had many serious handicaps to overcome besides a lack of experience and tradition. The majority of the British public had yet to be convinced that their own country-people could dance at all. Ballet to them meant the Russian Ballet, though they were quite willing to be taken in by the use of Russian names. They did not realise that the Russian dancer had suffered from a

[1] It was known as the Vic-Wells Ballet when first created.

Ninette de Valois (photograph by Anthony)
Frederick Ashton (photograph by Anthony)
Marie Rambert (photograph by Peggy Delius)
Constant Lambert (photograph by Anthony)

Miracle in the Gorbals

Celia Franca as the Prostitute

(Photograph by Edward Mandinian)

David Paltenghi as the Official, Robert Helpmann as the Stranger and Pauline Clayden as the Suicide

(Photograph by Edward Mandinian)

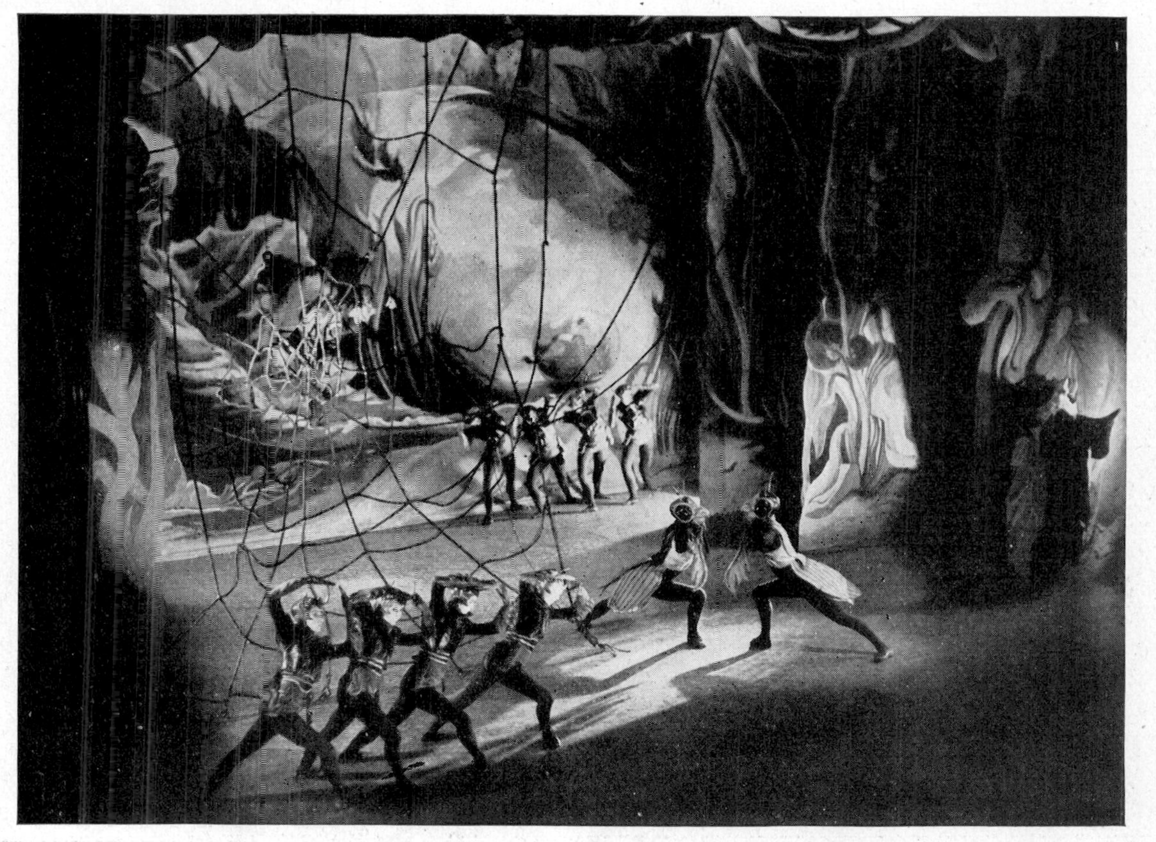

Le Festin de l'Araignée—Décor by Michael Ayrton. Celia Franca as The Spider

(Photograph by Edward Mandinian)

Le Lac des Cygnes—Décor by Leslie Hurry. Act 1. Robert Helpmann as Siegfried, Joy Newton as the Princess

(Photograph by Tunbridge-Sedgwick)

Le Lac des Cygnes—Act 3. Robert Helpmann and Margot Fonteyn

(Photograph by Tunbridge-Sedgwick)

Spectre de la Rose—Margot Fonteyn and Alexis Rassine

(Photograph by Anthony)

Hamlet--General scene. Décor by Leslie Hurry

(Photograph by Tunbridge-Sedgwick)

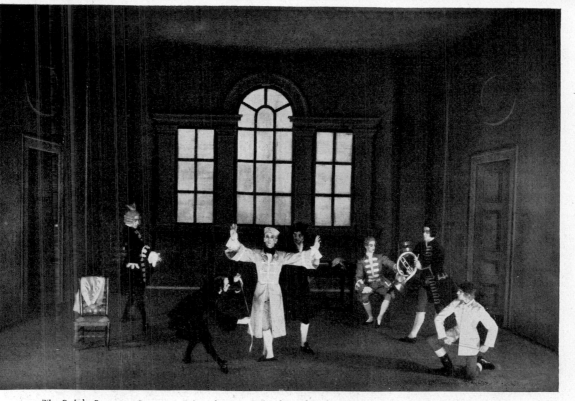

The Rake's Progress—Scene 1. Décor by Rex Whistler, after Hogarth. Robert Helpmann as the Rake

(Photograph by Tunbridge-Sedgwick)

Comus—Décor by Oliver Messel. Scene 2: Margot Fonteyn as the Lady; Robert Helpmann as Comus

similar handicap at the end of last century, when the Italian alone could delight balletomanes with her brilliant *fouettés*.

The reverse of the medal was the obstinate chauvinism of a certain section of the public that praised every effort extravagantly just because it was national. The task of the pioneers of English ballet was to produce good ballet irrespective of nationality, to avoid pandering to any form of artistic snobbery. The Anglo-Russians formed a bridge on which both parties could meet, a solid bridge engineered by Diaghileff himself. The test would come when that bridge was withdrawn and with it the magic of a name; only a name, because the Diaghileff influence would in fact persist.

British ballet was born at Sadler's Wells when Alicia Markova (1935) withdrew to lead a company of her own. During her reign, and the word is rightly chosen, it had been Markova and a worthy background, a repetition on a smaller scale of Pavlova and company. The public flocked to the out-of-the-way theatre in Rosebery Avenue to applaud Markova, both in her creations and in the revivals of the classics, *Giselle*, *Swan Lake*, *Casse-Noisette*.

When Markova left a whole company took the place of a star, a company trained in the theatre school, a company with a distinct personality of its own. It is a common mistake to think that a company cannot exist without a ballerina; it is in fact a far healthier state than a ballerina with merely a background and no company. For several seasons, until Margot Fonteyn grew to full stature, Sadler's Wells had no ballerina. Its strength lay in its skilled direction, in the promise of its young dancers, in its own personality. No sooner was it founded than it had to fight fierce rivalry from visiting companies, most notably Colonel de Basil with his dazzling constellation and his Diaghileff heritage. The reasons for its survival will be seen when we analyse the war years in detail. English team-work played its part, but would not of itself have been sufficient. The clue was brilliant management and the work that went on unnoticed in the school. Russian visitors had the immense Diaghileff repertoire to draw upon; Sadler's Wells was compelled to create, and to revive the pre-Diaghileff classics. Sadler's Wells shared one advantage with Diaghileff, the leisure to create. While de Basil was conquering America with his yearly tours of some hundred cities in six months, the English company was performing twice a week, just as Diaghileff had done at Monte Carlo. In this way a repertoire was created and one that contained few errors; for with the repertory system a ballet company aims at something like permanence for every creation.

The basis of the Wells' success in its creations was sound musical planning. The fashion of Russian ballet since 1933 was the danced Symphony: Tchaikovsky 5th, Brahms 4th, Beethoven 7th. This the English company rejected for a variety of reasons: the timing of the Symphony made its use unsuitable to ballet, its structure made for monotony and repetition. It was, in fact, a blind alley. Constant Lambert, conductor of the Camargo, conductor and musical adviser of Sadler's Wells, built up a repertoire of brilliant musical arrangements, suitable for theatrical dancing, yet with an existence of their own. For the first time Russian (*émigré*) ballet was at a complete musical standstill and it was the English company through Lambert that had truly inherited the Diaghileff tradition. Musically *Les Patineurs*, *Les Rendezvous* and *Apparitions*, arrangements of Meyerbeer, Auber and Liszt can stand alongside *La Boutique Fantasque* (Rossini) and *Schéhérazade* (Rimsky-Korsakov). The specially commissioned music by a Stravinsky, a Ravel or a Walton is an exception; ballet still depends for sixty per cent of its repertoire on the selection and arrangement of already existing music. Without Lambert's skill in musical repertoire-building, Sadler's Wells could not have survived the war. The performance of a series of danced Symphonies would never have formed the basis of a permanent repertoire.

Equally important as the creations, from many points of view more important, are the revivals of the classics. With Markova as an inspiration, and later with their own Fonteyn, Sadler's Wells revived the classics in their entirety. *The Sleeping Princess*, Diaghileff's great London venture of 1921, since then only seen in its one-act version as *Aurora's Wedding*, *Coppélia*, *Giselle*, *Casse-Noisette* and the full version of *Swan Lake*, taught both public and dancers the meaning of choreographic classicism. By special arrangement with Fokine those masterpieces of neo-romanticism, *Les Sylphides*, *Carnaval* and *Le Spectre de la Rose*,[1] were included in the repertoire, examples of ballet at its most sensitive and subtle. This solid foundation formed the education of a generation of dancers and their public, it gave the new company an academic standing and a tradition, the indispensable means of survival.

II. SADLER'S WELLS PRODUCTIONS, 1939–1944

1. *The Background*

With the outbreak of war the demand for ballet steadily grew, partly no doubt from escapism, since ballet is the last stronghold of theatrical illusion, but mainly through the need for *re*-creation in the Greek sense of the word. Since 1939 symphonic music, opera and the plays of Shakespeare have all enjoyed an outstanding success, greater by far than the temporary rubbish compounded of farce and swing that is the true product of escapism. This war has shown that the average theatrical manager has in the past consistently underestimated public taste.

So great was the prestige of the Sadler's Wells Ballet in 1939, in spite of its headquarters in an unfashionable part of London, that many letters were written to the papers, among them one by Bernard Shaw, suggesting that the few male dancers should be exempted from conscription, as their absence would jeopardise the existence of something precious for national artistic prestige in the future and useful for public morale in the present. Very wisely the management did not identify itself with this plea. To have done so, whether with the slightest prospect of success or not, would have damaged ballet beyond recovery in the public mind. The male dancer has yet to earn the complete recognition in England that he has in Russia. His true function as a virile partner contrasting with the ballerina, whose fragility and beauty reveals and enhances, has yet to be fully understood. The fact that the male dancers of Britain's ballet not only opposed all pleas

[1] Today these works are often mistakenly called " classics ", and the mistake is a dangerous one that Fokine always insisted upon correcting. They were created deliberately as a revolt against classicism.

for exemption on their behalf, but as volunteers and conscripts enjoyed an exceptionally fine record in all the services, while it added greatly to temporary difficulties, will, I am convinced, go a long way towards banishing any prejudice against male dancing and bringing the right type of boy to ballet. Every one of the original male personnel of Sadler's Wells was in the Forces. As soon as a boy learnt to play his part in the company he left. This meant constant rehearsal with immature youths but it was well worth while.

It is not my purpose here to stress the many war-time difficulties and dangers suffered by the company. The artistic record is the important thing and it needs no excuses. Many of these difficulties were common to the theatre in general; the dangers were shared on both sides of the footlights. Dancers performed and audiences applauded during the worst aerial bombardments, often when other theatres, and cinemas, were empty. On one occasion members of the company fought an incendiary bomb fire and saved the theatre; it was all in the day's work in 1940–1941.

But one experience in particular deserves special mention. In May 1940, under the auspices of the British Council, Sadler's Wells went on a goodwill tour to Holland. (They returned to Holland in January 1945.) They had just given their fourth performance of the tour, at Arnhem, when the Germans invaded. Their bus, a few hours ahead of the panzers, reached the Hague in safety. And there they waited during anxious days of bombardment and street fighting. The last boat carried them out, minus scenery, scores, costumes and personal belongings, but ready, without an interval, to carry on with their work.

They made many tours of England during the Battle of Britain, two pianos replacing the orchestra. They produced new works, danced to soldiers, sailors, airmen and factory workers. Then when the clouds lifted they found their orchestra once again and settled in a west-end London home, the New Theatre. And nightly they filled the hall. Crowds waited for hours in the street, through rain, air-raid warnings and raids. In 1944 they moved to the Princes Theatre, one of the biggest in London. All this is the background to the main story of artistic development.

In 1939 Sadler's Wells Ballet was known to an enthusiastic group in London who found their way three times a week to an out-of-the-way theatre. For a few weeks in the summer it visited the larger provincial centres. By 1944 it was known all over Britain and it performed nightly. In 1939, only 45 per cent of the company were products of the school; in 1944, over 85 per cent; for the school too carried on.

During the period 1939–1944 there were 12 creations and a classical revival on a large scale. In 1944 the total current repertoire comprised thirty-four works.

Statistics as a rule are dull, but these few are a necessary addition to the war background, if the intense creative urge of Britain's youngest art is to be understood.

But the critic's duty is to ignore the circumstances of production and to deal only with the results. More than ever in war-time, when there is no foreign competition, it is essential to maintain the highest critical standards. The following account seeks to bear those standards in mind.

2. *Ninette de Valois*

De Valois' work as a choreographer has been greatly restricted by her duties as director of the company, especially in war-time, when the difficulties involved are greater than anyone could believe possible when applauding the customary smooth performance.

De Valois' work has made Sadler's Wells and it is characteristic of her whole outlook that her one ambition is to see the foundation so solid that " no one will know the name of the director ". The work of de Valois, the director, does not in its detail concern the present study once its importance has been underlined; our present concern is with her artistic creations.

Job made her name; *The Rake's Progress*, the first Wells ballet with an English theme, assured her as a choreographer an important place in the history of the art. She has always succeeded on the heroic canvas in tackling something in the grand manner. Her less important productions have often been dull through the very excess of detailed and conscientious work she has put into them.

Dull, that is, to the average audience. The expert, score in hand, will always find points to admire in the beauty of her skilled craftsmanship.

In both *Job* and *The Rake's Progress* she translated for the stage the work of a painter. In the second case her *étude de mœurs* was a perfect picture of the eighteenth-century England of that great satirical painter, Hogarth. To this, in her first war-time production, she added a companion piece.

The Prospect Before Us, 1940, only falls short of *The Rake's Progress* in one particular; its action, a story of back-stage intrigue in the London of the late eighteenth century, is a trifle too complex for easy narration. On the other hand, since it concerns a company of dancers, the dancing proceeds perfectly naturally. The inspiration was the work of the English water-colourist Thomas Rowlandson, the inventor of a whole gallery of grotesque characters of the England of some half a century after Hogarth.

In their different media Hogarth, Rowlandson, and Charles Dickens through his illustrators, give a detailed commentary on English social history from the age of Dr. Johnson to that of Queen Victoria, stressing in the typically English manner the eccentricities that we have always appreciated, and underlining the dramatic contrast between beauty and the beast. Theirs is a black-and-white world which avoids half-tones, and they are essentially theatrical in their outlook.

Once again de Valois has entered whole-heartedly into the spirit of the period and created some real characters, in particular the bibulous Mr. O'Reilly, a clown in the grand manner, admirably played by Robert Helpmann. Her knowledge of the ballet of the period makes an entertainment which is also a first-class document. Once again with her scholarly use of fine material, and a rich and large contrast, de Valois has made a complete success.

The music by the eighteenth-century English composer William Boyce selected by Constant Lambert is admirably wedded to its subject, and Roger Furse has freely translated the paintings of Rowlandson to re-create the London of 1789. Particularly interesting and novel is the artist's use of a drop-curtain to carry on the narrative in a manner impossible in the ballet medium. His cloth shows the fire at King's Theatre and the resulting panic, a canvas full of character and movement.

It is to be hoped that this is but the second work in a trilogy, the third of which will reproduce the England of Dickens via Cruikshank and Hablôt Browne, his illustrators. De Valois, Irish by birth, Russian in her ballet training, is the most English of all choreographers.

Her next ballet, *Orpheus and Eurydice*, 28th May 1941, was an experiment in presenting Gluck's opera as a ballet with solo voices, respecting the original libretto but returning Eurydice to Hades in the end, thus restoring to the legend its original tragic significance.

Mythology, once so popular a hunting-ground for the choreographer, has rarely been successful in modern ballet. Fokine, in spite of Ravel's brilliant score, failed with *Daphnis and Chloe*; his *Narcisse* was also a failure, and only Nijinsky's *L'Après-midi d'un Faune* remains, a fragment, largely on account of its original treatment *en profil* and the *succès de scandal* of its first presentation. De Valois herself had previously tried with *The Origin of Design* (Handel) and Beethoven's *Prometheus*. The latter was full of subtle points that showed a master knowledge of the score, but it failed to please. *Orpheus and Eurydice* met very much the same fate. Perhaps in all these cases the pattern of music does not lend itself to balletic narrative, certainly not to the dramatic development of character. Only the completely stylised mythology of Ashton's *Pomona* with Lambert's score has held a Sadler's Wells audience.

De Valois' third war-time ballet, *Promenade*, 1943, was a complete success in an idiom new to her, the small canvas that exploits the charm of pure dancing.

Its music is an arrangement of airs by Haydn admirably suited to the story of a butterfly collector, pursuing his hobby in a park, oblivious of the life and the flirtations that go on around him. In atmosphere it is a counterpart to *Carnaval* and *Papillons*, an admirable opening ballet, which the repertoire previously lacked. British ballet has always excelled in the strong dramatic *ballet d'action* rather than in the ballet of atmosphere and charm. Ballet is to folk-dance what the vintage wine is to the *vin du pays*. In *Promenade* Ninette de Valois has drawn with great skill on the

Breton folk-dance, which she learnt for the purpose from a soldier of the F.F.I. The scenery and costumes have been designed with great skill by Hugh Stevenson, a young artist who has already contributed a great deal to our ballet and who excels in romantic setting and costume at a period when the accent is largely on the grotesque.

3. *Frederick Ashton*

I have written about Ninette de Valois with intense pleasure. I shall write about Robert Helpmann with equal pleasure, but the case of Frederick Ashton is different. With the first two, words are easy to find; not so with Ashton. That already tells us something of his work. De Valois is a painter of conversation pieces; one can put those pictured conversations into words. Helpmann deals with various theatrical problems; one can state those problems and examine how he has dealt with them. Ashton just makes his people dance. He is a Braque who reaches emotion through form and colour. To explain Ashton it would be necessary to nudge the reader during an actual performance, to point to some movement, to draw his attention to the music. Then it would be unnecessary to say anything at all. He would know how exactly right and how moving that particular passage was. Ashton's work is the furthest removed from literature. Many writers have interpreted his ballets with an enormous wealth of expression that has amazed Ashton himself. As he has a particularly caustic tongue I have no intention of following suit.

Ashton was born in Ecuador and it is certain that Spanish melody and colour have affected his temperament. That can be seen in many of his early works; *Rio Grande* is too obvious an example on account of its subject. I have briefly outlined his career in the introductory chapter. His was an entirely natural gift that flowed with such ease that without hard study it might easily have remained stationary. It started along original lines, then with the beginnings of popular success became a trifle derivative and superficial, finally to develop into the work of a master choreographer in the great European tradition. Ashton's range is

The Wanderer—Décor by Graham Sutherland
(Photograph by Anthony)

The Quest—Backcloth for the Magician's Cave by John Piper

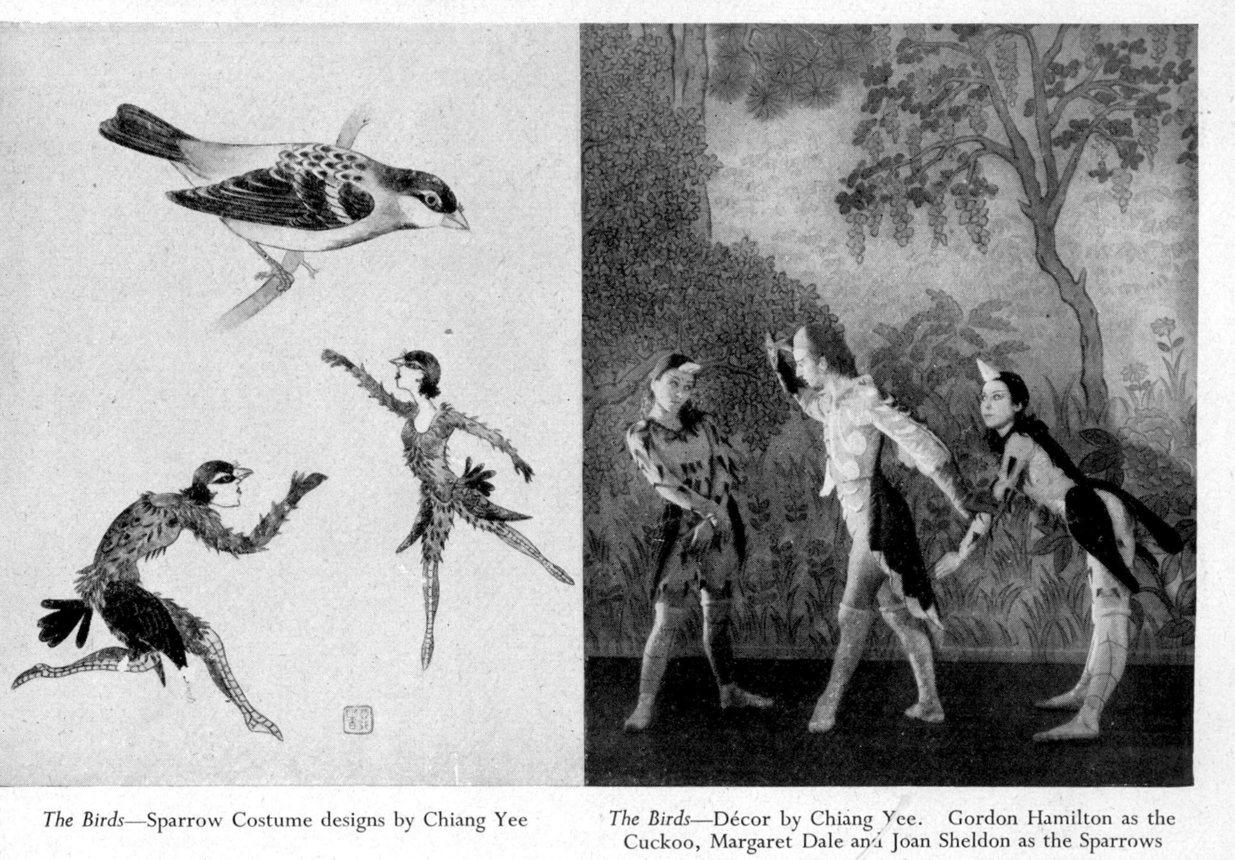

The Birds—Sparrow Costume designs by Chiang Yee

The Birds—Décor by Chiang Yee. Gordon Hamilton as the Cuckoo, Margaret Dale and Joan Sheldon as the Sparrows

(Photograph by Tunbridge-Sedgwick)

Hamlet—Costume design for the Ghost by Leslie Hurry

Hamlet—Alexis Rassine as the Ghost, Robert Helpmann as Hamlet

(Photograph by Tunbridge-Sedgwick)

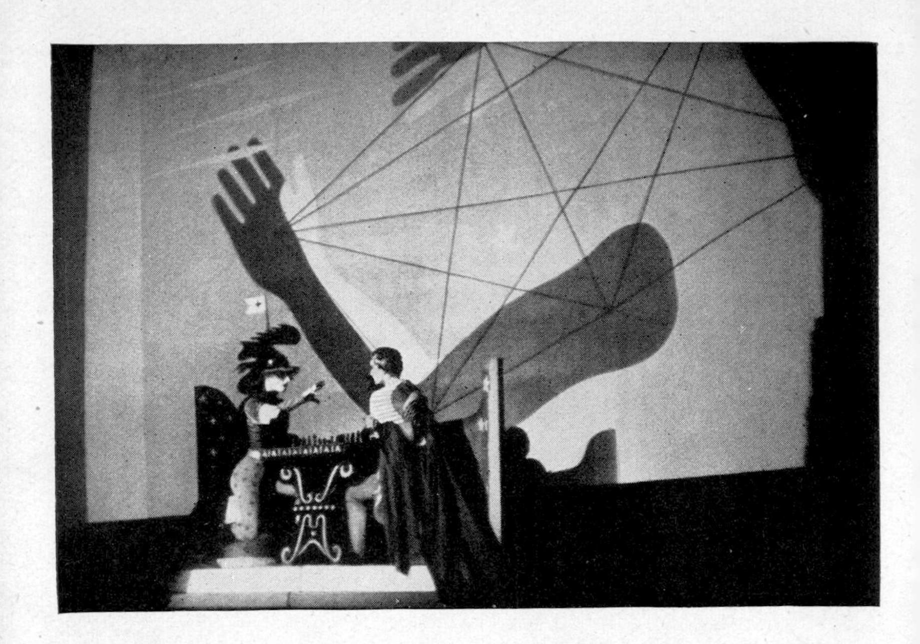

Checkmate—Décor by E. McKnight Kauffer. Prologue: Love—Joy Newton; Death—Frederick Ashton

Checkmate—Michael Somes as the Black Knight

(Photographs by Peggy Delius)

surprisingly large; broad humour in *Façade*, sophistication in *A Wedding Bouquet*, true romanticism in *Apparitions*, elegance in *Les Rendezvous*. No one has enriched the British repertoire to such an extent.

Ashton's war-time creations have been few. From 1941 he held His Majesty's commission in the R.A.F.

His first war-time ballet was written in a mood of intense indignation and revealed a new Ashton. *Dante Sonata* is Ashton's heartfelt protest at the rape of Poland. There is no obvious symbolism, no draped and labelled figures, but there can be no mistaking the choreographer's intention. Patterned by the music Ashton shows the struggle between the powers of good and evil, revealing in a bitter and dramatic finale that both are crucified, even when the good triumphs.

That is a brief explanation but, as I have already made clear, it is quite impossible to explain an Ashton ballet away from the music. This ballet is tremendously exciting. Ashton, who had previously excelled in the tender *adagio* or the witty variation, handles a group like a romantic painter, a Delacroix mixing colour.

A feature of British ballet has always been the evocation in scenery and costume of the work of some painter; Blake in *Job*, Hogarth in *The Rake's Progress*, Rowlandson in *The Prospect Before Us*. In this case Sophie Fedorovitch, who has so many times collaborated with Ashton, has evoked the sculptor-draughtsman Flaxman (1755–1826), known the world over for his designs for Wedgwood's ceramics. The choice is highly significant in an Ashton ballet. It would be difficult to find a less literary artist.

It was always a firm belief of Serge Diaghileff that the music of Bach was unsuited to ballet, and with one exception experience has proved him right. The exception is Ashton's ballet, *The Wise Virgins*, and is clearly due to the selection and amazingly skilled arrangement of Bach by William Walton, which presents the music in a form suited to narrative and climax. The story is the familiar biblical parable with its humour, tenderness and possibilities of character contrast. It has been given a Renaissance setting, the work of the late Rex Whistler, a master of décor, killed in action in 1944. Ashton has accordingly based his movements on the work of Italian masters. This seems comparatively easy when one remembers the rich material available. It is in fact the most dangerous task that any choreographer could undertake. It needs a master touch. What is easy is to produce a few carefully selected groups that will make at least one member of the audience exclaim excitedly, "Look! how clever, that's just like the picture by Fra Something-or-other we saw in Florence." But Ashton has thoroughly digested his material and the result is a Quattrocento exhibition. It is more than that; it has a rich humanity.

Ashton's *The Wanderer* is a choreographic pattern set to the music of Schubert's *Wanderer* (Liszt's arrangement for piano and orchestra). There is no plot. It is Ashton's reaction to the music, just as *Choreartium* was Massine's reaction to Brahms' 4th Symphony. Many critics have hailed it as Ashton's greatest work. There can be no argument. It depends upon their own personal reaction to the music and discussion is vain.

The scenery and costumes were entrusted to an abstract artist of great distinction, Graham Sutherland. Once again criticism must be purely subjective. The understanding of the great role that the abstract artist can play in such a work is important and may lead us far in the future. De Basil was a pioneer in that direction with André Masson's setting for *Les Présages*. The majority of the public, although accustomed to non-programme music, have yet to accept the logical partnership of the abstract painter.

Frederick Ashton's fourth war-time work, *The Quest*, was produced during a special leave, granted him for the purpose by the Air Ministry. It is essentially a national work, based on a legend of England's patron saint, St. George, from Spenser's *Faerie Queene*. The score, one of the most distinguished in the ballet repertoire, was the first specially written for ballet by William Walton, and the decorative work is by that great modern romantic, John Piper. It is a magnificent piece of team-work, but the action is a trifle too complex to produce the finest results. Ashton is seen at his best with a very simple theme, with the development of moods and atmosphere. In *The Quest* one can see his fine craft, and there are some subtle touches in his characterisation of the Seven

Deadly Sins, but it lacks the seeming spontaneity of his greatest works.

The national theme must never be forced for an occasion in a national ballet. The Russians produced only one *Petrouchka*: a fact that should always be borne in mind.

The finest tribute paid to Ashton while rehearsing *The Quest* came from a newcomer in the *corps de ballet*. "I did enjoy working for Ashton. I felt I was learning and improving the whole time."

He is the dancer's choreographer.

4. *Robert Helpmann's Ballets*

Robert Helpmann started his career as choreographer in 1942 after many years of experience as a leading dancer and an actor on the dramatic stage. He came to the Sadler's Wells Ballet School in 1933 from Australia, one of the many who had been inspired by a visit from Pavlova. It is characteristic of Ninette de Valois that when she saw him the very first thing she said was, "I can do something with that face." Helpmann is the born actor.

It was natural that with his outlook and dual training he should try to find a new direction for ballet; he has found three.

His first ballet was a modification of an early English art form, the Masque, in which movement, music and the declamation of poetry are blended, usually in a pastoral setting. The masque was as native to England as ballet to France and opera to Italy, but it died with changing social and political conditions. Helpmann took the most famous of these masques, Milton's *Comus*, 1634, produced it as an ordinary ballet, but retained two speeches which he recited himself in the title-role. These speeches were introduced with great skill, causing no break in the action, in spite of the change of medium. The story of *Comus* is highly balletic. Comus himself is a Pan-like creature, conceived by Milton as a son of Circe and Bacchus, who has enslaved through their love of pleasure and over-indulgence a group of men and women who have grown the faces of beasts and monsters. He attempts to make a new victim, a young girl whom he woos in the guise of a shepherd. Then he shows himself in his true colours and tries to tempt her. She is rescued by her brothers, who are led to the spot by a guardian spirit. The story is admirably direct and the contrast between the pure young girl in white and the gaily-coloured masked monsters is a dramatic one. Oliver Messel, designer of scenery and costumes, has entered into the spirit of this enchanted forest, and his décor succeeds in being a part of the drama. Constant Lambert has selected and lightly orchestrated music by Purcell, correct in period and so dramatically appropriate that it might have been written for the purpose.

In Britain ballet is taken by many in deadly earnest, discussed, argued over and analysed by clubs that have sprung up in every large centre, and particularly in University towns. This very guarded return to a bygone tradition caused something of a sensation. Heated debates occurred as to the justification of the use of speech in ballet and as to where it would lead. The discussion was largely irrelevant. Since the days of the masque actors and dancers have become specialists—too much so. Helpmann remains an exception. Speech, even if the dancer were trained, would certainly destroy ballet as we know it, bringing it so close to the dramatic stage as to be indistinguishable from the expressionist play. It is not only a question of aesthetics but of breathing. Even in *Comus* Helpmann's actual movement was drastically curtailed by his need for the breath to recite. He was already the actor, not fully able to join in " the light fantastic round " to which he summoned his rout of monsters.

Helpmann's first mood was that of the antiquarian; his next revealed him as a literary critic of the advanced modern school. He set out to give a balletic interpretation of Hamlet.

Here one must distinguish him from other choreographers who have laid hands on Shakespeare; there is a recent example in *Twelfth Night*. It should be obvious that there is no virtue in a Shakespearian story as such. Shakespeare himself received them at second hand. You or I might have written a dozen such plots. Without the language of Shakespeare they are without significance, *Hamlet* without the Prince of Denmark. Also, in most cases, they are too complex to make suitable ballet scenarios.

Helpmann is too good a theatre man to use the name Shakespeare as a magic talisman. He has acted in Shakespeare and already, while arranging his ballet of *Hamlet*, was making a close study of the character which he acted at the New Theatre in 1944. The action of his ballet is based on the words

> For in that sleep of death what dreams may come
> When we have shuffled off this mortal coil,
> Must give us pause.

The scene starts with Hamlet at the moment of death. His life is then recapitulated in a feverish dream as events pass through his memory like a drowning man, and the curtain falls at the same point where it rose. In this delirium his character is given a Freudian interpretation. This form of criticism is admirably suited to the ballet medium. Visually it is even more effective than when put into words. Hamlet's confusion between Ophelia and his mother, his jealousy of Laertes, can be convincingly shown in the dance.

This work more than any other illustrates the true role of décor and costume in ballet, not as an embellishment or a background but as an integral part of the drama. The music is Tchaikovsky's Overture, a romantic work, but Helpmann's action is essentially modern in outlook. There is no clash between the two because they are reconciled in the scenery and costumes of Leslie Hurry, a modern romantic painter. Hurry, whom Helpmann discovered as a stage designer through an exhibition of his work, also redecorated the great classic *Swan Lake* with conspicuous success. He may prove to be the British Bakst.

After they had generously applauded *Hamlet*, and in particular Helpmann's interpretation of the title-role, the analysts got busy once again. "This is all very well," they said, "but is it ballet at all? There is so little dancing in it."

Here they showed a lack of understanding of modern ballet as stated and created by Michael Fokine, who laid down that everything in ballet is dancing except the conventional *hand-on-heart-means-I-love-you* mime of classical ballet; even the raising of an eyebrow must be guided by the music not merely in tempo but in spirit as well. An opera parallel will make this clear. In opera there is the *aria* or song and there is the *recitative* or narrative. Both are recognised as singing. Exactly the same is the case in ballet. There is the set dance, the *adagio* or variation, and " *recitative* " or " narrative " dancing, which is exploited by de Valois and more especially by Helpmann.

However false the reasoning of the analysts, it seems to have stung Helpmann to an immediate retort. His next work, *The Birds*, was an exercise in orthodox ballet technique. The plot was of the conventional farm-yard variation, and dealt with the flutterings and flirtations of birds, the heroine obviously being a nightingale, the comic relief a hen. The music was an arrangement of old melodies by the Italian composer Respighi, an amusing score but almost too illustrative to be altogether a success. An original note was introduced by the decorations of a Chinese painter, Chiang Yee, whose birds were treated with fine skill and originality and whose scenery mitigated the banality of the subject.

The ballet was neither a failure nor a success. The technical complication of the dancing, particularly in a *pas de quatre*, was at times so great that smooth performance was difficult. Only with the entrances of the hen did we catch glimpses of the true Helpmann. One missed the easy flow of an Ashton in a subject that was particularly his. Helpmann showed his proficiency in the classical idiom and that was all. He confounded his critics, but lost his way in so doing.

Miracle in the Gorbals, Robert Helpmann's fourth work, presents an entirely new departure in ballet, a realistic dance-drama in a squalid contemporary setting. Kurt Jooss in his *Big City* shows very much the same scene but his action is stylised while Helpmann's is brutally real. Moreover, to a greater extent than ever before, the characters are seen in the round, they cannot be labelled white or black, good or bad. They develop with the situation and, as is so rarely the case in ballet, the plot really matters and grips the audience. It is a simple plot of universal appeal, one that has lent itself to the masterpiece of a Dostoievsky in *The Grand Inquisitor* or to the successful melodrama of a Jerome K. Jerome in *The Passing of the Third Floor Back*. It tells of the reappearance of Christ in the modern world, His reception by man and the church and His new martyrdom. The subject, in spite of its attractiveness, is full of pitfalls. Unless treated with a reverent sincerity it can easily prove offensive, also it lends itself to a mawkish sentimentality. A measure of Helpmann's success is that this ballet has offended no section of the public and has been welcomed with enthusiasm and understanding by the ecclesiastical press, who see it as a new and powerful morality play.

The setting for this great dance-drama is the Gorbals, a slum in Glasgow, once notorious for its lawless gangs, its overcrowding, poverty and despair. Its inhabitants are the riff-raff of any great port, the characters of a Gorki's *Lower Depths*. The one diversion of their young people is dancing, the fierce competition for cup or medal at the Palais on a Saturday night as they slide and gyrate to a hot American number. And deep down in them is the feeling of race that can be brought to life by the skirl of the pipes, that can make them forget the Charleston and remember the reel.

Dance-drama depends entirely for its success on whether the narrative is direct enough to be told without speech, without the need to refer to voluminous programme notes, read in the dark by aid of a match to the annoyance of all one's neighbours. It also depends on the choice of a setting; whether it has in it elements of the picturesque that can be naturally developed. In the present case both story and location are admirable; the drama is vivid and direct, the protagonists almost a primitive people, quick to anger, quick to compassion, easily awed and with a background of pipes and reels that can penetrate through the walls of their artificial surroundings.

But there is an added complication. We are not discussing a mimed play but a dance-drama that must be a perfect collaboration between music and movement both in structure and feeling. Arthur Bliss, whose *Checkmate* had shown him to be a master writer for the stage, has provided the ideal score, realistic in that he makes use with powerful dramatic effect of the wail of a ship's siren, but always with full musical justification. The skilled use of Scottish folk melody explains the background of the people. This score has the grand simplicity that the perfect stage music requires as an accompaniment to complex action. But the very word accompaniment is misleading; the music is the dramatic book, the very motive power of the whole ballet.

This story of the effect of the stranger's presence on a squalid community, and more particularly on a clergyman, a prostitute and a suicide, whom the stranger restores to life, might easily have been sordid had not composer and choreographer seen below the surface dirt and shown us moments of moving lyrical beauty. Two in particular stand out from anything in the previous record of ballet; the superstitious awe of this grimy crowd of individuals united in the presence of death and the effect on the resuscitated girl herself. At first as she opens her eyes and sees the stranger her joy is entirely spiritual, she has been reborn. Then as the warm blood runs tingling through her veins that joy becomes human and she breaks into a reel that she must have danced as a carefree schoolgirl. That is balletic subtlety, but it is obvious to the whole audience.

I remarked that the characters were " round " and developed. The clergyman, for instance, who opposes and finally delivers the stranger to death, is not just a bad man, he is a strong man with all the possibilities for good or evil. He is a sensual man ashamed of his own sensuality. The more one analyses this work the more one realises its closeness to a novel in its mass of detail, yet it is always plastic and never literature at second hand as the commentator is forced to make it appear.

The third partner, décor and costume, is one with music and movement. Edward Burra has seen the hidden beauty of the slum. His dockside drop-curtain suggests the mysterious spiritual voyage that can be made from this forbidding spot.

The fine acting that this work receives from the company underlines the speciality of British dancers who have been trained in the rigid convention of classical ballet. They showed the same ability in de Valois' *Rake's Progress* and in *The Prospect Before Us*.

Does this point to the future of British Ballet? There are many dangers ahead, if that is so. Only a dancer-actor of Helpmann's experience could have tackled the difficult problems with such sureness of touch. I have seen many ballets with a message, social or political. They have been for the most part drab and pretentious. Helpmann, while utterly sincere, was concerned not with the message but with its aesthetic presentation. That must be clearly understood.

In four works, all produced during the war years, he has tackled three distinct and difficult problems greatly enriching the whole dramatic scope of ballet. But he has done so as a brilliant individual and it would be dangerous to follow up any of his discoveries and make a school of them. Frederick Ashton (with his brilliant discoveries of line and movement) remains the schoolman of British Ballet.

5. *Other Productions*

Choreography has always been the major difficulty in ballet production. There is no scarcity of talented dancers waiting eagerly for the steps to dance.[1] A school can form a dancer, but there can be no school for the choreographer, who must develop his natural gifts through experience. In his quarter-century of artistic activity Diaghileff used Fokine, already developed as a choreographer, and "discovered" Nijinsky, Massine, Balanchine, Nijinska and Lifar. At no time was it possible for him to have more than one resident choreographer in the company; he found choreographers by far the most temperamental of his artists. Our ballet has been fortunate in its team spirit that has allowed de Valois, Ashton and Helpmann to work together at the same time. A newcomer to the company has been the talented Andrée Howard, sensitive and most feminine of choreographers, who started her work and made her reputation with Marie Rambert, in particular with the fantasy *Lady into Fox*, the perfect miniature ballet.

The ballet she produced for Sadler's Wells was Albert Roussel's *Le Festin de l'Araignée*.

Choreographers have long drawn on the animal world for inspiration; the swan has become a symbol for the greatest of all ballerinas. Pavlova also made the dragonfly famous in the dance. A whole ballet, however, on the life-cycle of creeping, crawling things is a novelty.

[1] This is not an empty phrase. In my tour of dancing schools in June/July 1945 I have seen them.

The theme is a simple one.

A garden in the South of France. A spider makes ready her web, surveys the landscape and watches with grim anticipation the activities of the insects. After ensnaring several of these she prepares for her banquet, but is suddenly stabbed by a praying mantis who has escaped from her web. Night falls on the deserted garden.

The music for this Fabre-like programme was written by the French composer Albert Roussel, one of the many gifted pupils of Vincent d'Indy at the Scuola Cantorum.

Andrée Howard has treated her subject realistically and her insects are not just symbols. They reveal a subtle study of insect movement, and the rise of the curtain with the spider climbing up and down its gigantic web is thrillingly effective. It produces much the same shudder as the real thing. The audience has the impression that it is watching this drama of life and death through a powerful magnifying-glass.

The scenery and costumes play a very important role in producing this illusion, and the choice of the artist, Michael Ayrton, was a fine example of the Diaghileff method that has now become Sadler's Wells'; that of making the perfect choice of composer, decorative artist and choreographer, so that the ballet stands as a whole. *Le Festin de l'Araignée* is a fine piece of theatre.

The war saw two great classical revivals. *The Swan Lake* was redressed and decorated by Leslie Hurry, an important new discovery and a born theatre artist, who has combined romantic tradition with a new and very personal vision. Fokine's choreographic poem *Le Spectre de la Rose*, reproduced by Karsavina, was redecorated by Rex Whistler, his last work before he was killed in action. It serves to underline our great loss. He was the Benois of our movement.

6. *The Dancers*

A good company is a team with a personality of its own. In ballet the "star" system has no place; only the ballerina and her opposite number stand apart. *Ballerina* is a title to be earned through experience in the ranks followed by the skilled interpretation of the great classical roles. In countries where there is a state ballet that is clearly understood, but in England the term has often been abused to include anyone who is not absolutely in the *corps de ballet*. The ballerina is a rarity: Russian Imperial Ballet only produced five in a generation. Britain has one *prima ballerina assoluta*, Margot Fonteyn, trained at Sadler's Wells, a product of the system and a member of the team.

When that great Anglo-Russian Markova left, the company remained without a ballerina. Gradually Fonteyn began to emerge, first as a sensitive artist, then as an accomplished technician. Fonteyn is distinguished by an extraordinary musicality that gives her a wide range of interpretation from the severe classicism of Tchaikovsky's *Swan Lake* to the porcelain romance of Columbine in *Carnaval*, from the tragedy of *Giselle*, her greatest role, to the sly modern humour of Lord Berners' *Wedding Bouquet*. Fonteyn gives the most extraordinary detail to each role, building it up from performance to performance. Her Swanhilda in *Coppélia* is not merely the accomplished ballerina in gay mood but a complete character. In this range of characterisation she resembles Karsavina more than any other dancer.

In the opposite number to the ballerina, the *premier danseur classique*, Britain has not excelled. There are many candidates for the role, the most promising being Michael Somes and Alexis Rassine. Britain's leading dancer is the versatile Australian, Robert Helpmann, who by his skill as an actor and his feeling for style can assume the role of the *danseur noble* or the character part of Dr. Coppelius at will. Helpmann has the mask of the actor, as de Valois immediately recognised. His dancing technique is adequate, his stagecraft exceptional. He can fill the stage by his personality, he can also mime the smallest role without monopolising the attention. And the dance is but a part of a career that includes the dramatic stage and the films.

Fonteyn and Helpmann together have proved a unique combination.

It is impossible to characterise the entire company, but mention must be made of the deputy ballerinas, Beryl Grey, a dancer of noble line and effortless virtuosity, outstanding for her fine musical phrasing, Pamela May and Moira Shearer; also of Margaret Dale, Avril Navarre, Gillian Lynne, Julia Farron, Violetta Elvin, Gerd Larsen, Pauline Clayden and Anne Negus. Each has a well-defined personality that has finally disposed of the idea that the British dancer has discipline, technique and very little else.

Sadler's Wells ballet today is like a well-trained symphony orchestra, a sensitive instrument upon which the choreographer can play tragedy or comedy.

III. OTHER COMPANIES

1. *Marie Rambert and the Ballet Club*

We have seen how largely Marie Rambert and her group contributed to the success of the Camargo Society and, indeed, the whole story of British Ballet has been one of friendly collaboration where rivalry would have meant extinction. But at the same time she retained her individuality, starting the Ballet Club with its headquarters at the Mercury, a bijou theatre specially built for the purpose. There on a miniature stage she evolved an entirely new art form, *ballet de chambre*, consisting of small, sophisticated and exquisitely finished productions with results more rapid and immediately apparent than with the larger Sadler's Wells. This gave her the opportunity for experiment, and she fostered much choreographic talent in addition to that of Frederick Ashton already mentioned. Andrée Howard was perhaps the most successful with this new type of ballet, producing its *chef-d'œuvre*, *Lady into Fox*, an adaptation of David Garnett's fantasy, as well as half a dozen charming miniatures. Antony Tudor, today a leading light in North American ballet, made his début on her stage and produced for her two outstanding works, *Jardin aux Lilas*, now a major success in New York, and *Dark Elegies*. Frank Staff, a South African, and Walter Gore both created works for her and after being invalided out of the services are now with her once again.

Marie Rambert has lost many of her company both to Sadler's

Wells and the Russian companies, but has gone on with her pioneering work, and the war gave her opportunities of carrying ballet to places in England where it had never been seen before.

The war found her established at the Arts Theatre in the West End of London. There she played to packed houses throughout the bombardment of 1940–1941, giving as many as four performances a day. Then C.E.M.A. took a hand.

Those initials C.E.M.A. are a particularly welcome addition to the many new words formed during the war. They signify Council for the Encouragement of Music and the Arts and represent a happy British compromise in the question of a Ministry of Fine Arts. C.E.M.A.[1] is a non-political body with a Government grant and it operates by extending a helping hand to those artists who are already helping themselves and to the public hungry for art. As well as providing for big cities, C.E.M.A. sends concerts, exhibitions and theatrical companies to communities too small or isolated to guarantee a financial result and has thus guaranteed performances by all the leading ballet companies. In this way Marie Rambert has toured factories, hostels and small towns as well as appearing in London, and has spread a love of ballet in many hitherto remote districts.

But a mere recital of all this does not do her justice. She has not marked time artistically. Since the outbreak of war she has produced eleven new works, the most outstanding being Walter Gore's *Simple Symphony*, set to music by Benjamin Britten (produced a few months after Gore was twice torpedoed on D-day), Frank Staff's *Peter and the Wolf* by Prokofiev, and the same choreographer's *Czernyana*, a delightfully witty *suite de danses* to the well-known pianoforte exercises by Czerny.

The company's leading dancer, Sally Gilmour, is a sensitive artist, whose impersonation of the vixen-woman in *Lady into Fox* is one of the most notable dramatic contributions to contemporary ballet.

Marie Rambert's position in the history of British ballet is assured both by her development of chamber ballet and her discovery of talent. But it is likely that she has only written the

[1] Now called the Arts Council of Great Britain.

first chapter. Circumstances have made her excel on a small stage, but it is evident that this does not satisfy her ambition, especially as her artists after a time wish to seek their fortunes on a large stage, dancing to a symphony orchestra. Time will show whether she is able to expand, but her understanding of the classics, which she was the first to revive, makes a strong case in her favour.

Marie Rambert's invention of chamber ballet, originally imposed on her by necessity, but later developed into a true art form, has given rise to a school and she has had many followers, the best known of which were the London Ballet, founded shortly before the war by Antony Tudor, and Keith Lester's Arts Theatre Ballet. These two groups shared with Marie Rambert the Battle of Britain seasons at the Arts Theatre and, given the circumstances, produced some good work. The devotion of the artists deserves high recognition. The Ballet Guild has also produced chamber works, but its main importance lies in the future. The *London Archives of the Dance*, of which Cyril Beaumont is the chairman, was founded on 9th January 1945, and is an organisation similar to the famous *Archives Internationales de la Danse* in Paris.

2. *The International Ballet*

Extraordinary evidence of the hold that ballet has on the British public was the formation in 1941 of a new company on a large scale, the International Ballet.

During its short existence the International has mounted fourteen productions, seven of which are revivals of the classics, redecorated by such artists as Rex Whistler and competently reproduced. The guiding spirit of the new enterprise is a talented young dancer, Mona Inglesby: director, leading dancer and choreographer. This may possibly be too heavy a burden for any one person, and experience has shown that management and dancing are a particularly hard combination.

Among the creations are *Everyman*, an attempt to give in ballet form but with sparing use of the voice the celebrated morality play. The costumes by William Chappell and Rex Whistler's décor are among the most beautiful in contemporary ballet, but Mona Inglesby, in spite of interesting ideas, has been handicapped by the selection of the music, an arrangement of symphonic poems by Richard Strauss that does not blend with the subject and that is unfortunate in itself. *Twelfth Night*, a balletic version of Shakespeare's play by Andrée Howard with a delightful setting by Doris Zinkeisen and music arranged from Grieg, is a charming entertainment, but the story without Shakespeare does not lend itself particularly well to ballet, and the literary instead of the musical or plastic approach is always a dangerous one, leading in the long run not to ballet but to wordless drama.

The International is too young as yet to discuss in detail as a company, but its directors have taken the best means of securing quality and permanence by starting their own ballet school, 1944. Meanwhile they have done much in bringing the classics to audiences all over Britain at a time when such calm sane beauty is a necessity.

3. *Kurt Jooss, Welcome Guest of Britain*

The Ballet Jooss is not a British product but it has found a home in England, material support and a public of its own.

Kurt Jooss first formed his company in Essen. He visited France, England and America with his remarkably prophetic work *The Green Table* and rapidly established a reputation as an original thinker with a new contribution to make to ballet. When Hitler came to power there was no room in Germany for so independent and sensitive an artist and friends made it possible for him to make his headquarters in Britain. The war found the Jooss Company touring the United States. In 1942 C.E.M.A. brought him back to this country and ensured his future; a fine service to contemporary art irrespective of the country of its origin.

Kurt Jooss does not belong to classical ballet. His technique is a compromise between the work of Laban and ballet proper, that does not admit the use of the points of the toes. Jooss aims at a form of dance-drama and is especially interested in sociological themes. His company is a magnificently disciplined team, especially strong in male dancers. Against a background of curtains on a stage lit by a master and well costumed his cast interprets his ideas so completely that it is difficult to single out any one person; the company itself is the expression of Kurt Jooss.

Jooss, using a minimum of virtuoso technique, is a master of vivid narrative and at his finest when he has something important to express, as in *The Green Table* or his recent *Pandora*, a symbol of present-day life. In the trivial anecdote, such as his recent *Company at the Manor*, one can feel the lack of the lightness to be found in the orthodox technique. Only in *Ball in Old Vienna* does he show all the charm of Lanner's Valses and their period.

The case of Kurt Jooss, late of Essen and now an honoured artist in this country, is a significant one that needs no comment.

4. *The Royal Academy of Dancing*

Unperceived by the theatre-going public there is a vast dancing profession training pupils to take their place on the stage, or at any rate to acquire more grace and understanding of ballet in general. These teachers have trained other teachers until every centre in Britain has its dancing school. There is no law to prevent anyone opening a school and giving it a high-sounding and pretentious title, and in the past many unqualified persons have done so, often distorting the limbs of their unfortunate victims. Today the Royal Academy of Dancing, under the presidency of Adeline Genée, who inspired more than one generation of British dancers, keeps a watchful eye over the profession, giving its certificate to teachers it deems competent and holding annual examinations for pupils of those teachers. The Academy has also many valuable scholarships to award; the Leverhulme is for £150 per annum for three years and ensures the recipient one year with the Sadler's Wells Ballet.

Since 1939 the work of the Academy has gone on unchecked, and not in this country alone. It has sent examiners yearly to Canada, South Africa, Australia and New Zealand, who have braved the dangers and discomforts of war-time travel to maintain the high standard of teaching. Its record, unknown to even our own general public, is astonishing. In 1943, for instance, in

Pamela May as the Young Girl in *Nocturne*

(Photograph by Edward Mandinian)

Beryl Grey in *Le Lac des Cygnes*

(Photograph by Anthony)

Jardin aux Lilas—Ballet Rambert production. Choreography by Antony Tudor

Dark Elegies—Ballet Rambert production. Choreography by Antony Tudor

(Photographs by Peggy Delius)

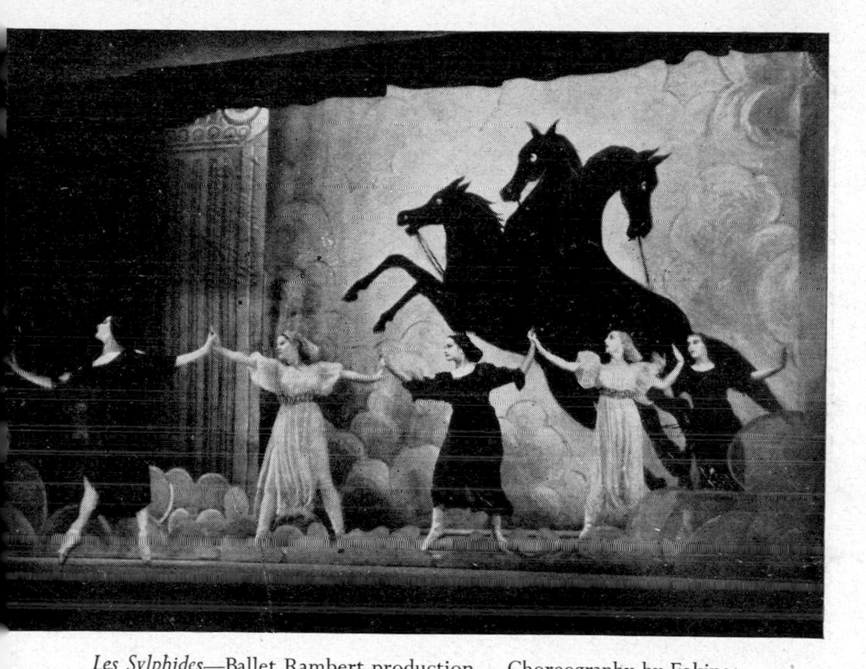

Les Sylphides—Ballet Rambert production. Choreography by Fokine; décor by Ronald Wilson

The Descent of Hebe—Ballet Rambert production. Choreography by Antony Tudor; décor by Nadia Benois

(Photographs by Peggy Delius)

Margot Fonteyn as Odette in *Le Lac des Cygnes*

Robert Helpmann as Dr. Coppelius

Great Britain alone, some twelve hundred girls were examined in major examinations and over twelve thousand children in elementary exams. The entire scholastic profession is interested in this work and is in close touch with the Academy. The Academy has its own Production Club, a valuable training ground for the young choreographer and dancer. Truly the British are once more a dancing nation.

5. *Other Activities*

This does not completely cover the activity in Britain during the war years. The period bristles with small and shifting companies; associations of dancers eager to let off steam, glorified pupil shows, managers seeking to exploit the craze, as well as small groups of idealists bringing ballet to hostel and factory. Some of these companies have died after a season or two, others will fade away as soon as foreign companies can supply the demand. If creatively they have done little to serve ballet, they have played their part in providing entertainment.

A company that has given great pleasure to many is the Anglo-Polish Ballet, an offshoot of the Polish Ballet founded before the war exclusively for the exploitation of national themes. Since 1939 the Anglo-Polish Ballet has been almost a hundred per cent British in personnel. It has excelled in the gay and colourful peasant dances inherited from its purely Polish predecessor and has thus justified its name.

Some mention must be made of the Ballet Club movement, associations of *amateurs* who discuss and put on their own productions. Liverpool before the war was a pioneer and since 1939 Manchester and Edinburgh have done good work. There are now a dozen such clubs.

IV. NATIONALISM IN BALLET

1. *British Dancing*

It is obvious from the foregoing account that ballet is now indigenous to Britain. The period under review has been particularly rich in creations. There is no doubt of the public demand.

We now come to two important questions: Is there an English style of dancing? What direction is British ballet taking?

France, Italy and Russia have each in their turn powerfully influenced the dance and ballet itself—always remember that the dance is but a fourth part of ballet—in a manner that it is easy to assess. The Russian Academy was founded in the middle of the eighteenth century, but the Russian style, so perfect a combination of French grace and Italian virtuosity, only fully emerged at the beginning of the present century.

That gives us an answer to our first question. It takes several generations of assimilation to develop an easily recognisable style of dancing that can be given a national label, and national physique, temperament and environment will undoubtedly produce such a school in time. Our Russian-named British dancers are purely Russian in their technical approach and method of attack, as is also our first ballerina creation, Margot Fonteyn. But it is already possible to divine certain characteristics.

The British are an athletic people and their dancers are quick to learn. That very speed may be something of a handicap since their work in general lacks the extraordinary precision and finish of the contemporary Russian State dancer. The British dancer is exceptionally musical—one can surely feel the influence of Constant Lambert—and not only can cope with difficult rhythms but has a feeling for nuances that the present-day Russian dancer, more of a virtuoso, somewhat lacks. The British attack is altogether softer and as yet no British dancer can so completely dominate the large Opera House stage as did a Trefilova yesterday or an Ulanova today. On the other hand, there is less of an extreme between *corps de ballet* and principal, and the team spirit is very noticeable. In the definite dramatic character role the British dancer has no equal and such balletic acting is instinctive. It is impossible to imagine in spite of the choreographer's meticulous care that every member of the large cast of *The Rake's Progress* understood the England of the eighteenth century, yet each role was superbly acted and the whole was made up of innumerable vignettes. In *Miracle in the Gorbals* each dancer, from the newest recruit to the principals, acts with a detail and yet a restraint that shows the gift to be inborn. The crowd scenes in *Petrouchka*, the greatest of all Russian dramatic ballets, have for a very long time consisted of what were only too obviously walkers-on; in British ballet there are no walkers-on, all are actors who contribute to the complete picture. This is perhaps understandable. The British are temperamentally undemonstrative and welcome the chance of hiding themselves in a strong dramatic role. Where they largely fail is in the delicate romantic atmosphere of a *Sylphides*—Margot Fonteyn being an exception in that respect. The British dancer is positively unhappy—and here we must make an exception of Helpmann—in the old-fashioned miming of such a classic as *Swan Lake*. This may give us some clue to the British contribution to dancing. Fokine stated that in modern ballet there was no separate mime, that the dancer must be expressive from head to foot, that every gesture was a part of the dance. The British dancer may bring that ideal very close to fulfilment.

But there is another side to the problem, a physical as well as an aesthetic aspect. It would be possible for the expert to walk into the classroom and to know immediately whether he is watching Italians, French or Russians by their movements alone. Could he distinguish a British class ? The answer to that is definitely no. Our actual teaching has yet to strike out a line of its own, and that can come through time but never through deliberation. Ballet is an art of tradition in which progress comes through evolution but never through revolution.

2. *British Choreography*

Our second question as to the direction of British ballet as a whole is altogether easier to answer and, indeed, our study of recent ballets has partly answered it. Temperamentally we favour the conversation piece, the dance-drama, but a new conception of that dance-drama so often discussed and attempted in Central Europe as a reaction from classical ballet. Our dance-drama is entirely classical in its technical foundations and the classical ballet will always serve as an inspiration to our dancers and their public.

We have realised the truth of Diaghileff's constantly asserted dictum that ballet technique was a means and never an end. This realisation has made all forms of modern dance technique unpopular with our dancers and public.

The dance-drama in its crudest form has a standard basic plot, good versus evil, the plot of the old morality play, of most films and of very many novels for that matter. But our literature, especially the great novels of the Victorian era, while usually imperfect in form and in plot, have always excelled in characterisation. As a nation, in spite of the fact that we are considered hide-bound in tradition and that our education tends to turn out a definite type, we value eccentrics and even admire their foibles. The heroes and heroines of Dickens are colourless, his eccentrics have become part of our language and ourselves; the same applies to Walter Scott. British ballet is taking a similar line. Its dance-drama is not merely putting a story on the stage but is exploiting character to the full. Ballet has always known the standard figures of the *Commedia dell' Arte*, but the characters in our type of ballet are not flat and static, they undergo development with the action, and the action itself depends on that development. *The Rake's Progress* by its very nature is a morality play in which the characters are largely stereotyped; in spite of that de Valois has succeeded in giving them life. *Miracle in the Gorbals* is also a morality play but the characters are as subtle as in a drama or a novel. They are real people, no longer the puppets of conventional choreography. De Valois' chessmen in *Checkmate* are faced with Nemesis, but as they struggle they awake our sympathy because they are real; we identify ourselves with the aged Red King, feeling for and with him. Ashton's foolish virgins are so many Doras out of *David Copperfield*, yet Ashton in his approach is the most international and the least British of choreographers.

British ballet, like the British film, is moving to a more realistic point of view, to narration and to the depicting and development of character, and as long as this avoids the purely literary approach it provides an inexhaustible field of opportunity. So far the guidance of Constant Lambert has maintained the essential relationship between music and action and the literary pitfall has been avoided. It remains a danger.

Finally a national ballet does not exist merely to exploit national themes. An unrestricted diet of roast beef and Yorkshire pudding would soon grow monotonous. Such themes arise naturally out of the environment and can never be forced. Excessive chauvinism kills art. Manifestations of nationality are far more subtle than dancing wrapped up in a Union Jack. In his long career Diaghileff produced only one *Petrouchka* but to the connoisseur *Les Sylphides* is equally Russian.

3. *The Future*

The war interrupted many carefully laid constructive plans which may be set down here as a future programme.

De Valois realised from the first that the school was the motive power of her company. She also realised what so many in this country have not yet seen, that the dancer to be a true artist and not merely a clever acrobat must be a well-educated person. Sadler's Wells school will become, when circumstances permit, a residential educational establishment with a proper curriculum that will bring the pupils up to matriculation standards. This will attract much fresh material to ballet and guard against the prevalent danger of the immature dancer who attracts the public for a season or two by her youth and enthusiasm and then fades out before these can be replaced by a conscious artistry.

In the future Sadler's Wells will entrust one work a year to a young choreographer by way of experiment and will also engage the services of an experienced foreign choreographer to mount certain works that should be included in a well-balanced repertoire. This will guard against the dangers of excessive insularity.

The company will travel and during its travels will gain ideas from the countries it visits. There is, for instance, a quality of valuable artistic material in the Dominions unknown in this country. Ballet has caught on there just as at home. Australia is in the process of forming a national ballet; Canada, South Africa and New Zealand have ballet clubs. These young countries are rich in themes and have already given to the Russian Ballet [1]

[1] Denisova, Lvova (Canadian).

and to Sadler's Wells [1] and other companies many fine dancers. The possibilities for artistic exchange within the Commonwealth are endless and have not yet been touched upon.

In this country itself the war has brought about a welcome decentralisation. For the first time premières of importance are given outside London and every big city has its flourishing Ballet Club. Through its own Production Club the Royal Academy of Dancing will form a link with these so that all talent has its opportunity. In this way the Academy will complement the admirable technical work that it has done.

Yes, the day when Miss Smith could only gain applause as Smithova has gone and once again a visitor will be able to say the English excel in dancing and making music.

[1] Robert Helpmann, Gordon Hamilton (Australian), Frank Staff (South African).

APPENDICES

APPENDIX A

The Artistic Pedigree of British Ballet

Ninette de Valois and Marie Rambert, main architects of British ballet, whose pupils form the bulk of the movement, studied under Enrico Cecchetti (1850–1928), who studied under Giovanni Lepri, pupil of Carlo Blasis (1803–1878)—s. under Gardel and Dauberval—s. under Noverre (1727–1810)—s. under Dupré—s. under Pécourt (1653–1729)—s. under Beauchamps (died 1704)—who was first *maître de ballet* of Louis XIV's Académie de la Danse, 1661.

APPENDIX B

Some Key Dates in History of British Ballet

1910 First London appearance of Pavlova
1911 First Diaghileff season
1912 Hilda Munnings joins Diaghileff under the name of Lydia Sokolova
1920 Founding of Association of Operatic Dancing
1923 Ninette de Valois joins Diaghileff
1924 Anton Dolin joins Diaghileff
1925 Alicia Markova joins Diaghileff
1926 Ninette de Valois opens her Academy of Choreographic Art
1929 Death of Diaghileff
1930 Opening of Camargo Society
1930 *Formation of Marie Rambert's Ballet Club*
1931 *Formation of Sadler's Wells Ballet*
1933 Robert Helpmann joins Sadler's Wells
1935 Alicia Markova leaves Sadler's Wells
Margot Fonteyn, pupil of its school, emerges as principal dancer
1936 Association of Operatic Dancing becomes the Royal Academy of Dancing
1939 Sadler's Wells gives Gala at Covent Garden in honour of President Lebrun
1940 Sadler's Wells visits Holland
1945 Sadler's Wells returns to Holland and visits France and Belgium

APPENDIX C

Creations of British Ballet, 1939–1944

SADLER'S WELLS COMPANY

Classical Revivals

Coppélia (in its entirety)
music Delibes—costumes and setting William Chappell, 15th April 1940

The Swan Lake
music Tchaikovsky—new costumes and setting Leslie Hurry, 7th September 1943

Fokine Revival

Le Spectre de la Rose
music Weber—new décor and costumes Rex Whistler, 1st February 1944

Creations

By Frederick Ashton

Dante Sonata
music Liszt (arranged Lambert)—décor and costumes Sophie Fedorovitch, after Flaxman, 23rd January 1940

The Wise Virgins
music Bach (arranged Walton)—décor and costumes Rex Whistler, 24th April 1940

The Wanderer
music Schubert—décor and costumes Graham Sutherland, 27th January 1941

The Quest
music William Walton—décor and costumes John Piper, 6th April 1943

By Ninette de Valois

The Prospect Before Us
music William Boyce (arranged Constant Lambert)—décor and costumes Roger Furse, 4th July 1940

Orpheus and Eurydice
music Gluck—décor and costumes S. Fedorovitch, 28th May 1941

Promenade
music Haydn (arranged Edwin Evans)—décor and costumes Hugh Stevenson, 25th October 1943. (First produced in Edinburgh)

By Robert Helpmann

Comus
music Purcell (arranged Lambert)—décor and costumes Oliver Messel, 14th January 1942

Hamlet
music Tchaikovsky—décor and costumes Leslie Hurry, 19th May 1942

The Birds
music Respighi—décor and costumes Chiang Yee, 24th November 1942

Miracle in the Gorbals
book by M. Benthall, music Arthur Bliss—décor Edward Burra, 26th October 1944

By Andrée Howard

Le Festin de l'Araignée
music Albert Roussel—décor and costumes Michael Ayrton, 20th June 1944

BALLET RAMBERT

By Andrée Howard

Carnival of Animals
music Saint-Saëns—décor Andrée Howard, 26th March 1943. (At the Mercury Theatre, London, before an invited audience)

The Fugitive
music Salzedo—décor Hugh Stevenson, 16th November 1944. (At the Royal County Theatre, Bedford)

By Frank Staff

Czernyana
music Czerny—décor E. Swinstead-Smith, 5th December 1939. (Duchess Theatre, London)

Peter and the Wolf
music Prokofiev—décor Guy Sheppard, 1st May 1940. (The Arts Theatre, Cambridge)

Enigma Variations
music Elgar—décor Guy Sheppard, 26th November 1940. (The Arts Theatre, Cambridge)

Czerny 2
music Czerny—décor E. Swinstead-Smith, London, 15th May 1941. (Arts Theatre)

By Walter Gore

Bartlemas Dances

music Holst—costumes William Chappell, 13th May 1941

Confessional

music Sibelius—costumes A. Howard, 21st August 1941

Simple Symphony

music Benjamin Britten—décor R. Wilson, 29th November 1944. (Theatre Royal, Bristol)

INTERNATIONAL BALLET

By Mona Inglesby

Planetomania

music Norman Demuth—décor and costumes Doris Zinkeisen, May 1941

Everyman (production Leslie French)

music R. Strauss (arranged E. Irving)—décor Rex Whistler; costumes William Chappell, 13th July 1943

By Andrée Howard

Twelfth Night (production Mona Inglesby)

music Grieg (orchestrated E. Irving and J. Clifford)—décor and costumes Doris Zinkeisen, May 1942

By Angelo Andes

Danses Espagnoles

Suite to music by Mantis, Castillo, Albeniz, Turina, Espert, da Falla—décor and costumes Hein Heckroth, 1943

By Harold Turner

Fête Bohème

music Dvořák—décor and costumes Beryl Dean, May 1941

also new productions of Swan Lake, Giselle, Les Sylphides, Carnaval, Coppélia, Prince Igor, and Aurora's Wedding

APPENDIX D

SADLER'S WELLS COMPANY

British Composers whose Works have been performed

Lord Berners—Arthur Bliss *—William Boyce—Hugh Bradford—Benjamin Britten *—Delius—Norman Demuth *—Edward Elgar—Gavin Gordon—Gordon Jacob—Constant Lambert *—Purcell *—Vaughan Williams—William Walton *

* Since 1939.

BRITISH PAINTERS RESPONSIBLE FOR DÉCORS

John Armstrong—Michael Ayrton *—John Banting—Cecil Beaton—Vanessa Bell—Lord Berners—Hedley Briggs—Edward Burra *—W. Chappell *—Roger Furse *—Derek Hill—Leslie Hurry *—Oliver Messel *—John Piper *—Francis Rose—George Sherringham—Hugh Stevenson *—Graham Sutherland *—Rex Whistler *—Doris Zinkeisen *

APPENDIX E

BIBLIOGRAPHY OF BOOKS ON BRITISH BALLET PUBLISHED SINCE 1939

1941 Gordon Anthony
Margot Fonteyn
(23 camera studies, and an appreciation by Eveleigh Leith)

1942 Gordon Anthony
The Sadler's Wells Ballet
(47 camera studies and an appreciation by Eveleigh Leith)
P. W. Manchester
Vic-Wells, a Ballet Progress

1943 Arnold L. Haskell
The National Ballet
Caryl Brahms
Robert Helpmann
(a study with photographs)

1944 Janet Leeper
English Ballet
(16 plates of costume and scenery designs in colour and a monograph)

1945 W. J. Turner
The English Ballet
(Monograph in Britain in Pictures Series. Coloured plates and photographs)
Gordon Anthony
Ballerina
(Further studies of Margot Fonteyn)

* Since 1939.

We wish to thank the *London Archives of the Dance* for carefully checking the particulars noted above.

FILMS SINCE 1939

Sir Laurence Olivier in "Henry V"

DILYS POWELL

FILMS SINCE 1939

THE period since 1939 has made history in British films. The war created a need for a kind of film never before made in this country—records of current history designed to perpetuate great events in our national struggle, and to inspire the nation by showing a picture of the day-to-day heroism of members of the armed forces, and of civilians in their many and varied war jobs. Under this pressure of necessity, documentary and war films reached a standard never before attained. Together with this development came an increase of activity in other kinds of film-making. This essay is a brief account of virtually all the important work done in the film world during the war and immediately after.

Miss Dilys Powell is well known as the film critic of the *Sunday Times*. She is also a distinguished writer in other fields, her latest book, *The Traveller's Journey is Done,* describing her life in Greece to whose cause she devoted herself during the war years.

GREENWICH PUBLIC LIBRARIES
CHARLTON BRANCH LIBRARY

ILLUSTRATIONS

FILMS SINCE 1939

Every week in Great Britain roughly twenty-five million people go to the cinema. It is the chief urban entertainment; in cities and industrial centres it has long supplanted the theatre as the great popular recreation, and gradually it is gaining a hold over the country-side too, bringing its fantasies and its records of fact into mining villages, rural communities, into the tiniest hamlets and centres of country life. In Britain all classes go to the cinema: intellectuals, professional classes, artisans, workers, everybody from the Prime Minister to the mill-hand hurrying out of the Lancashire cotton mill in clogs and a shawl. The war has done two things for the British cinema. It has greatly extended the range of subjects dealt with by films. And it has brought films to new and varied audiences. But this has been a gradual process. At one time it looked as if the conditions of total war might mean the end of the cinema as an entertainment and an industry in Britain.

When, on 3rd September 1939, the air-raid sirens sounded immediately after Mr. Chamberlain's announcement of a state of war, many people felt that an end had come to the old ways of life. Nobody would care to go out in the evening in a black-out which was, at the start, complete. The population of the big cities suffered an immediate change in character; hundreds of thousands of children, often accompanied by their mothers, were moved from areas exposed to bombing to so-called safe areas. Places of entertainment closed their doors early; in any case transport for getting to a cinema and back again was severely curtailed. As for the production of films in Great Britain, it looked as if that might come to a stop altogether. Many British studios, in the early stages of the war, were requisitioned by the Government, some of them for use as storage depots; British actors and technicians were called up; the materials for film production were drastically cut. At least one leading London newspaper thought of dispensing with the services of its film critic: this, it said, was no time for such luxuries. The stages by which Britain came, while using all her vital energies on the business of war, to preserve the basic structure of a cultural life, lie outside the story of the cinema in war-time. Yet the cinema is concerned, for it was one of the earliest of the arts to react to the circumstances of war.

It was not long before the first excitement passed. Soon the frenzy of digging trenches in the London parks, filling sandbags, fixing black-outs and building shelters died down; with the end of September, the close of the German campaign in Poland, and the relapse on the Western Front into static warfare, it became apparent that the first winter was to be a time of preparation. People settled into a routine; their lives were restricted by the black-out and the early shutting-down of trains and buses, by the beginnings of rationing, by the duties of civil defence, in which so many were already playing a waiting part as air-raid wardens, firemen and rescue workers. But the need for entertainment revived: for entertainment and instruction, since there was a great need in Britain for all classes to learn what was expected of them, how they could adapt themselves in town and country to the new conditions in which they were living, how they could prepare themselves for the dangers ahead.

In the field of entertainment the position of the British cinema at the beginning of the war was far from easy. The public depended in the main on American films. American stars had captured the imagination of the romantic British public; Gary Cooper and Greta Garbo, James Cagney and Bette Davis, not the stars of English studios, were the names to conjure with. In London, French films and, to a smaller degree, the films of Soviet Russia attracted the discriminating; but with a few exceptions British films aroused no critical interest among the serious public, while to the masses who swarmed to the popular cinemas they were merely an inferior substitute for the American-made film. Isolated good British films, of course, there had been. The work of Alfred Hitchcock, great English master of the *macabre*, from " Blackmail " in 1929 to " The Lady Vanishes " in 1936, had shown what could be done in an English style. Anthony Asquith, son of the famous statesman of the 1914–18 war, had displayed in " Dance Pretty Lady " (from Compton Mackenzie's novel *Carnival*) a delicate romantic sensibility, and in " Pygmalion " (from Bernard Shaw's play) a genuine authority in the handling of the camera. Just before the war another young director, Carol Reed, was beginning to prove his talents: his "Bank Holiday", directed from a script by Rodney Ackland and Hans Wilhelm, beautifully held the balance between comedy and drama against a strictly English background. But there was no tradition of British films as there was a tradition of French ironic drama on the screen, or a tradition of American fast comedy. The national characteristics of the British, whether good or bad, had not been infused into a national cinema. Want of continuity in production had deprived script writers and technicians of opportunities for the natural development of talent. There was no school of British cinema, as there was of, let us say, German cinema. Not, that is to say, in fiction. In the documentary manner a school already existed.

In the late 'twenties a group of young men who saw in the cinema an instrument of social and scientific enquiry began making short films of fact. Among them was John Grierson, a young Scot using his talent at first on behalf of a Government Department, the Empire Marketing Board. Later, when the Empire Marketing Board came to an end, its film unit was taken over by another Government Department, the General Post Office. Finally, after the outbreak of war, the G.P.O. Film Unit, as it was called, became the Crown Film Unit, controlled by the Films Division of the Ministry of Information.

This official body was not the only group of documentary film makers. Some young documentary producers had for some time been making films sponsored by commercial enterprises or public utilities. The major gas companies, and the Petroleum Films Bureau, for instance, had engaged documentary producers in the 'thirties to make films on housing, nutrition, education, the control of insect pests. The political influence of these documentary films was generally Left Wing. Many aimed at opening people's eyes to the condition of the under-privileged. But many more were purely scientific; they examined, recorded, and left it at that. The results reached only a tiny section of the public. These films were rarely shown in ordinary cinemas. But what the producers were doing was extremely important. Their work was alive; it had its roots in the contemporary world, in contemporary society. Gradually a type of film peculiar to Britain evolved. John Grierson, Paul Rotha, Arthur Elton, Basil Wright, Harry Watt, Donald and John Taylor, Edgar Anstey, Mary Field, Cavalcanti—little by little their names and their achievements were to reach a wide public. John Grierson was to become Films Commissioner in the Dominion of Canada. One or two from their number were later to make fiction films; Harry Watt for one, Cavalcanti, a Continental director who had settled down to work in England, for another. In any case, by the beginning of the war the documentary movement in Britain was established. It had a tradition, it had trained and skilled workers, it had unrivalled experience in collecting facts and presenting an argument.

Obviously one of the first things the cinema had to do when war broke out was to record events. The newsreel companies, of which there are five in England, could record major events; they could not record the changing face of the whole country. Fine work was done by the newsreels; many cameramen risked their lives to cover battles on land and sea and in the air, some were killed or wounded. But to avoid overlapping, during the war the work was pooled, the five companies taking it in turn to send cameramen to the scene of action, and each company using the pool of material. In any case, the background, as opposed to the foreground, of war could not be dealt with. This was where the documentary producers came in.

At first their difficulties seemed insurmountable. In the first weeks of war everyone with a camera was, naturally enough, suspect. The documentary producers wanted to make their contribution to the war effort. They wanted to record the vast social changes which were coming over Britain, they wanted to put their knowledge of the cinema as a means of instruction and propaganda at the service of the nation. As often in Britain, things moved slowly. The Government, with huge problems to grapple, did not immediately recognise the enormous power of the cinema. Commercial companies which had sponsored documentary films withdrew their support; there was danger lest the documentary units might be dispersed.

It is difficult, separated as we are by the years of hardship and deadly peril, to recapture the feelings and emotions of the first autumn and winter of war in Britain. Looking back now, an oddly insular air overlies the six months from the end of the German campaign in Poland to the beginning, in Norway, of the Nazi drive in Western Europe. The British had not realised their own danger and the danger of Europe. Even their war films, in the early stages, were complacent: and an early propaganda film, " The Lion Has Wings ", showed, with a *naïveté* which makes one shudder today, a German air attack on London frustrated by the height of the balloon barrage. There was, however, a vague feeling that something should be done about presenting the British case to the world in terms of the cinema. A Government Department for the creation and dissemination of propaganda (and, incidentally, for the exercise of censorship) had been set up in September 1939. It was called the Ministry of Information, and among its divisions was one concerned with films. During the first months of the war, the Ministry was already being attacked in the newspapers. It was accused of failing to appreciate the propaganda value of films, of allowing the British case to go by default and British material and technicians to be wasted; and at the turn of the year Sir Kenneth Clark, Director of the National Gallery of pictures in London, and a man known for his sympathy with all contemporary forms of artistic endeavour, was put in charge of the Films Division. This change in leadership meant the beginning of a new creative spirit in Government film making, though the results were not immediately seen. In 1940 Sir Kenneth Clark was succeeded by Jack Beddington, a man with an understanding of the aims of the documentary movement and a feeling for the film medium; Beddington continued to guide the Ministry of Information Films Division throughout the entire war.

At the height of the struggle a vast number of officially sponsored films, instructive in almost every walk of life, was produced in Britain: films for the farmer and the housewife, for the factory worker, the soldier, the sailor, the airman. But in that first winter energies were directed chiefly to a general propaganda end: as it were, to the spiritual arming of the people. Short story films were produced to prepare the public mood; not only official films, for among the commercial companies, one studio, I remember, made a group of short cautionary tales warning against the presence of spies and the dangers of careless talk. Presently distinguished feature directors were to be employed in directing these short films: Anthony Asquith, for instance, and Brian Desmond Hurst, a young Irishman who, just before the war, had completed a brilliant essay in realistic fiction, " On the Night of the Fire ". By the spring of 1940 the Ministry of Information had a small group of films ready, made in collaboration with the French, the idea being to demonstrate Allied solidarity in unity of aims as well as arms. At the same time a short documentary film on the German air raid, in November 1939, on the famous Forth Bridge, was shown: " Squadron 992 ". The film, produced by Cavalcanti and directed by Harry Watt, described the training of barrage balloon crews and the part they played in guarding vital areas: its racy dialogue and the beauty of its camera work were startling at a period when Britain still had so little to show in the propaganda field.

But soon the complexion of the war was to change. By midsummer not only Norway and Denmark, but also the greater part of Western Europe, were to be overrun by the Nazis. With the fall of France, Britain was jerked suddenly into a sense of her danger. From now on the British were fighting for their lives. And in this isolated and desperate situation a new sense of urgency inspired the makers of British films also. In isolation a tradition was founded.

During the period from the summer of 1940 to the final German defeat in North Africa which once more freed the Mediterranean for British ships, Britain was a besieged country, constantly under the threat of air raids; the normal activities of life were carried on under the greatest difficulties, and to make a film at all was a matter of shifts and stratagems. The documentary film producers were among the first to react to the changed circumstances. Self-trained in persuasion, they became the interpreters of the British mood in war. One recalls, for instance, from the summer of 1940, a reconstruction of a tiny tragic episode: " Men of the Lightship ", the story of a lightship machine-gunned by a Nazi plane and its

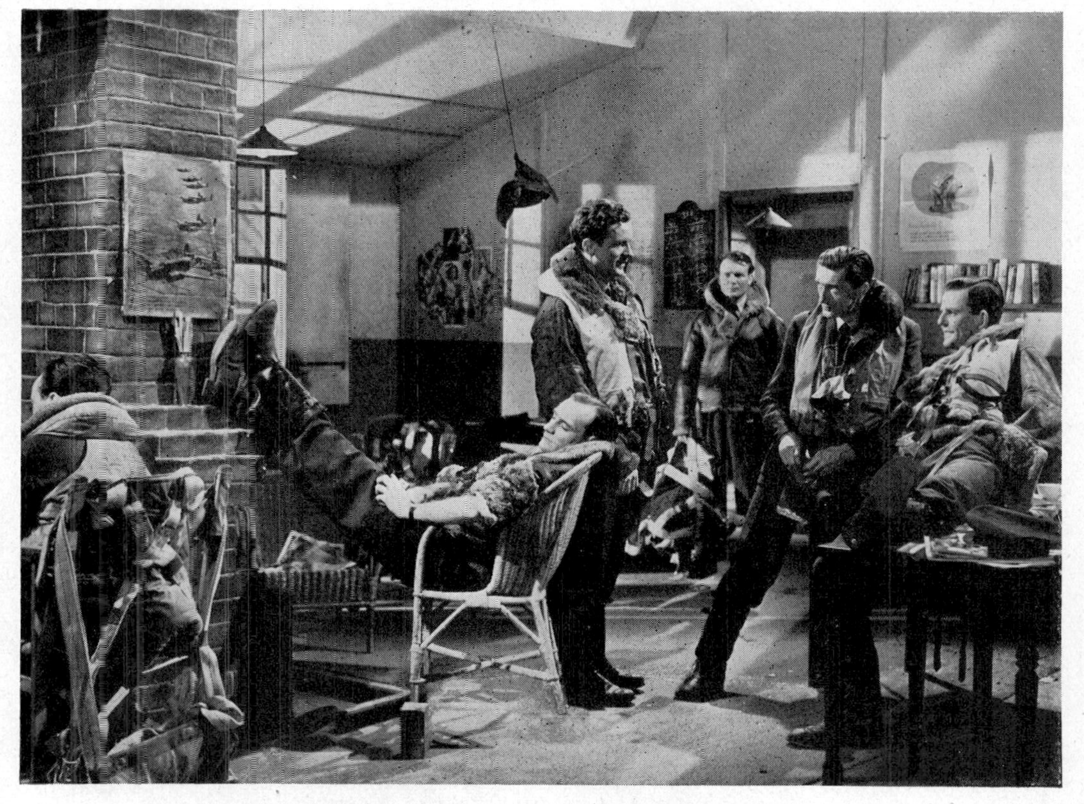

From " The Way to the Stars ", directed by Anthony Asquith

Allied Victory in the West : from " The True Glory "

Allied victory in North Africa : from " Desert Victory "

From Noel Coward's " In Which We Serve "

Paul Robeson in " The Proud Valley "

Above: Carol Reed
Below: Cavalcanti

Above: Humphrey Jennings
Below: David Lean

ANTHONY ASQUITH MICHAEL POWELL

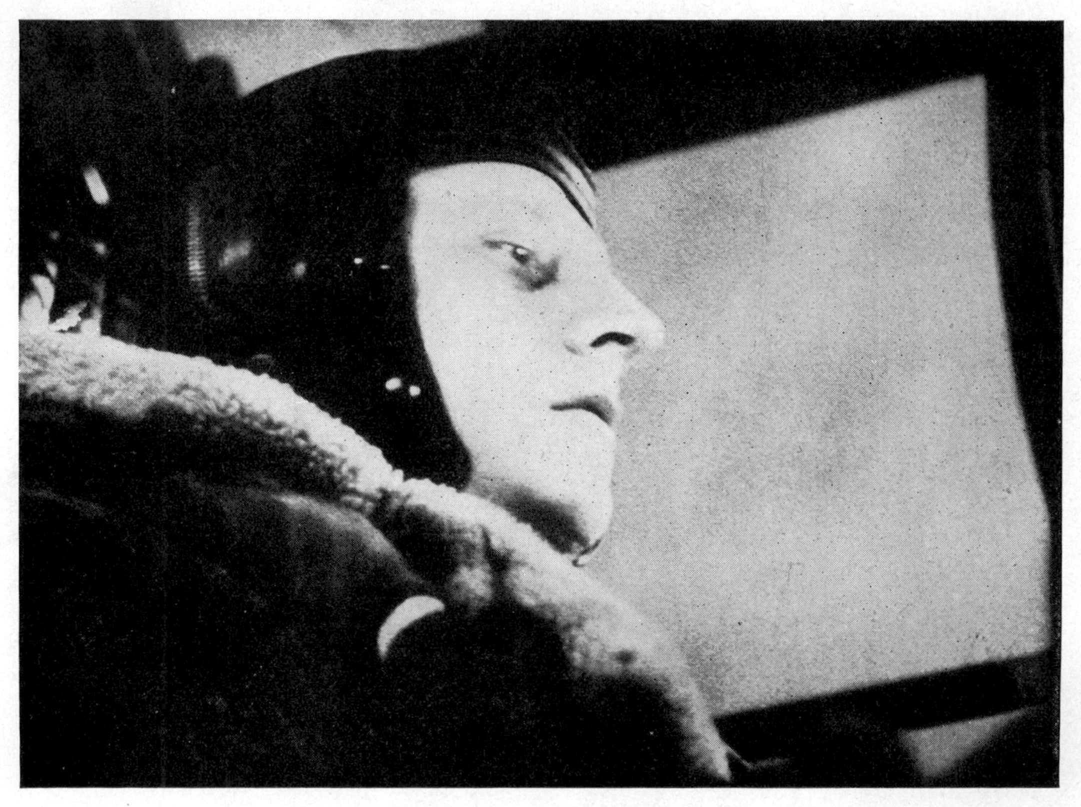

From the documentary film "Target for Tonight"

men left to row through days and nights until at last, when shore was reached, only one was left alive to tell the tale. "Men of the Lightship" was produced by a man from the documentary school, Cavalcanti; its director, David Macdonald, was a man from the commercial studios. Macdonald was to leave his mark on films even more strictly documentary: the fact is of importance, for it is evidence of the interchange that took place between commercial and documentary fields. But for the time being the young talents of the documentary movement kept mainly to their own side of the fence. That winter a little series of factual films, half newsreel, half pictorial comment, caught the public fancy. "Front Line", a record of life in the Channel Port of Dover under air raids and bombardment by long-range Nazi guns, was one of them. The most famous was "London Can Take It", a ten-minute picture of life in London during the great day and night raids of the Battle of Britain and the winter which followed it. The sirens in the darkness, the crowds moving calmly to the air-raid shelters, and the devastation of the morning after, with buildings shattered and city workers walking to their offices through streets littered with débris and broken glass—the story was moving and exciting even for those who knew it from daily and nightly experience. And its effect was sharpened by a commentary spoken by Quentin Reynolds, an American journalist, who praised the endurance of the London people and paid them a tribute which would have seemed fulsome for an English voice.

The skill of their editing and the effective use of commentary and dialogue, rather than anything essentially new in the method of narrative, gave these short films their success and, of course, their topical interest. Perhaps today we might find them a trifle embarrassing; the emotional tension of those days is gone, and now that the war is won we may not wish to be reminded of the spiritual excitement (for it was that) which enabled us to live through its worst moments. But in those days, to anybody who had experienced a night raid in a great city, the shots of London in darkness, and the crash of the guns, and the sight of the spires and domes and bridges still standing impassive next morning, were part of his very life.

But now a new element was to be introduced into the British documentary film: or rather I should say that an element already present was to be developed out of recognition. Many of us who before the war had seen in the British documentary school an integrity and a devotion to the task which promised more than we could find in the commercial cinema, had still been chilled at times by a want of humanity, of the poetry of human life, in the documentary output. Not always: Basil Wright in " Song of Ceylon " had achieved an incomparable pictorial lyricism; and Cavalcanti and Harry Watt in " North Sea ", a semi-documentary tale of a fishing trawler, had shown the ability to bring to the screen the drama of human character. In 1941 this ability was to be used by Watt to fresh purpose. " Target for Tonight ", the first and still one of the most famous of a series of British semi-fictional documentaries, was a reconstruction of an everyday happening in the war. A British bomber flies out, in the days when British bombers were few and small, to raid Germany. She is hit by flak, one of her crew is wounded, but somehow she struggles home. The actors were serving airmen, the dialogue was simple, realistic, ironic in the English manner. The whole setting was factual. But somehow imagination had irradiated a plain story of the everyday experience; the audience, excited and moved, shared the adventures of these young airmen who fought for them in such solitude and against such odds. Here was a new *genre* in the cinema: a fact, a fragment of actual life which still held the emotional tremor of fiction.

The *genre* was to be developed in the next few years: " Coastal Command ", directed by J. B. Holmes, a story of co-operation between shore-based aircraft and the Navy; " Fires Were Started ", directed by Humphrey Jennings, an episode from the great fire raids on London, superbly played by serving members of the war-time National Fire Service; all the list of semi-documentary war films down to the great experimental Technicolor piece, " Western Approaches "—with these Britain could indeed feel that she had made a fresh contribution, stylistic and technical, to the international cinema.

Meanwhile, notwithstanding the national peril, the social

documentary survived, and, indeed, matured. In the early months of the war directors and producers in this field were concerned, naturally enough, to observe rather than to point the way. The evacuation of children from the danger areas of London to districts where there were no military or industrial targets for enemy bombing; the problems of education with a population thus shifted; the life of a vast new army of factory workers, their tasks and their recreations—these were among the subjects which we find handled between 1939 and 1942. But just as, politically, the British were never content with the aim of military victory, so the documentary workers were not content with the recording of the face of war. There was a continual ferment in ordinary men's minds: they asked, not simply that the war should be won, but that it should be won to some purpose: that life after it should hold better opportunities. They asked it long before victory was certain; and it was not without justification that Churchill, badgered in some moment of desperate national peril by questions about war aims, brought the visionaries down to earth with " Our aim is to survive ". The keepers of the social conscience, the documentary workers, were among the most insistent of enquirers into war aims; and it is a tribute to the international outlook of the British that in 1943 a film was made, with the co-operation of many Government Departments, on the theme of universal food distribution. The producer, Paul Rotha, called his film " World of Plenty ", drawing, by the use of documentary and newsreel material, reconstructed episodes and recorded interviews, an ironic contrast between the plenty of the earth's fruits and the poverty of millions of the earth's creatures. The break-down in international food distribution before the war; the system of fair distribution by rationing enforced nationally during the war—from these premises a moral was drawn for the future. Another film made by Rotha, shorter, but worth noting for its content and treatment, was " Children of the City ", a study of juvenile delinquency in a Scottish city. Here the moral is driven home by a reconstructed episode: three boys break into a shop, are brought up with their parents before the juvenile court, which is a feature of the British judicial system, and are handled each according to his background and character—one given special treatment by child psychiatrists, one placed in the care of the local probationary officer whose business it becomes to see that the boy attends school and makes an effort at his own reform, the third sent to what in Britain is called an " approved school ", a school where young offenders are trained in useful trades and encouraged to take their place in a law-abiding society.

Parallel with these social documentaries ran a series of scientific and medical films. The Ministry of Information, for instance, produced, for the guidance of doctors, a film on the diagnosis and treatment of scabies. Another film dealt with the National Blood Transfusion Service, by which volunteers from all ranks of society gave blood to be stored and used when required for casualties, both military and civilian. But probably the most remarkable achievement among war-time medical films was the British Council's " Surgery in Chest Diseases ", a piece presenting with the strict beauty of science a delicate operation on the human lung. Here, in a film rightly acclaimed by scientists and doctors, the cinema performed a task impossible to any other medium: for by no other means could so accurate a view have been afforded to the public of the surgeon's duty and the surgeon's art.

Instruction in other fields was equally precise. As the war became more and more the battle of mechanics, of science and exact instruments, military, naval and air training grew more and more dependent on visual teaching; films were made which enabled the gunner to test the accuracy of his aim, which taught the airman the use of his controls. Much film production of this kind was kept secret from the ordinary civilian, and the end of the war did not immediately release more than a fragment of the material. The civilian, for his part, was kept informed on more general subjects. Tiny films lasting no more than two minutes, but often handled with irony and wit, were flashed on the screen in the intervals of entertainment films: they warned the spectator to economise in fuel and water, to note changes in food rationing, to collect salvage—waste paper for cartridges, household waste for pig food; and through a great part of the war the Ministry of Information presented each month a fifteen-minute film on the progress and significance of the struggle: on the fall and rehabilitation of Naples, for instance, on the devastation created in Walcheren by the flooding of the dykes.

Of the restrictions imposed on the newsreels I have already spoken. Yet the war was to bring a development of newsreel as well as documentary style. The Army, the Navy, the R.A.F., now employed their own camera units, who went into battle and took photographic records under fire. For three years the British had only scanty victories on land to record; Wavell's drive to Benghazi in 1940–41 did, it seemed at the time, little more than set the pendulum swinging in Africa; and it was not till El Alamein, in the autumn of 1942, that the great military subject presented itself. By 1943 the story could be told, and "Desert Victory", the work of Army and R.A.F. film production units, became the first of a series of full-length films of battle.

"Desert Victory", produced, directed and edited by two men trained in the entertainment film, David Macdonald and Roy Boulting, brought, to a public hardened to disappointment and waiting, a shock of triumph. The film, which recorded the advance from Alamein to Tripoli, included a small proportion of reconstructed shots and some captured German material. But the main story was told in direct factual sequences, elucidated now and then by diagrams. The painful pause before battle was joined, the preliminary bombing, the rout of the German army—at last audiences, stirring excitedly in British cinemas, felt the sense of national power. Technically, "Desert Victory" was remarkable for its editing: an unwieldy mass of material had been reduced to a coherent narrative. Emotionally it gained by its single-mindedness: here was a statement of victory, with a beginning, a climax and an end. Its successor in the following year, "Tunisian Victory", lacked something of this single-mindedness, partly, I think, because its producers were not in complete agreement on their object. "Tunisian Victory", which carried the story from the North African landings of November 1942 to the annihilation of the German forces at Cape Bon, was made jointly by British and American service film units: and all the mathematical care expended on a just division of film footage between American and British operations could not eradicate a certain feeling of indecision about the whole production, of faltering between military narrative and pious humanitarian hopes. The third in the series of Victories, " Burma Victory ", shown only after the end of the war against Japan, reverted to British direction, though it incorporated American material. And here once more the combination of factual material shot in the battle area with occasional reconstructed shots and diagrams gave an extraordinary directness and immediacy to the narrative.

From 1942 onwards, Russian war films had made a great impact on English audiences. " One Day of War in Soviet Russia ", " The Defeat of the Germans Near Moscow ", " Leningrad Fights ", " The Story of Stalingrad ", " The Battle of the Ukraine "—the drive and ferocious purpose of these Soviet documentary records had excited admiration and sympathy in London cinemas (they were not widely shown in the British provinces). Not many British war films were of a size to stand up to the Russian pieces. But " Desert Victory " could stand the comparison; so could " Burma Victory "; and when, after the German defeat in the West, British and American film teams combined once more to produce a battle record, many people felt that in the result even the Russian factual cinema had been left behind.

" The True Glory ", the story of the war in Western Europe from the Allied landings in Normandy to the ultimate Nazi collapse, was compiled and edited by two distinguished film directors, one American, one British. The American, Garson Kanin, was known before the war as a witty and tender director of romantic comedy, a man using the camera with a freedom rare even among the most successful of Hollywood talents. The Englishman, Carol Reed, has already been mentioned as one of the promising talents in the English cinema; during the war he was to prove his ability by a group of successful entertainment films. The two directors, quick, ironic, profoundly in sympathy with the ordinary fighting man, set to work on their apocalyptic story not simply as a stupendous battle scene, but also as the common experience of an army of human beings. The commentary was not merely interpretative, it was creative. By the device of letting the fighting man speak for himself in his own accents, by letting the audience hear the voice, resigned, exasperated, debunking, of the American and the Englishman, the farmer and the clerk, the city fellow and the countryman from the mountains, the war was made to appear, not some impersonal cataclysm, but a shared human experience. And a shared international experience: for the speakers were not only British and Americans; they were French and Poles, Norwegians and Belgians, Canadians and all the other fighters in the Western Army. " The True Glory " thus remains not as a historical document only, but as a human document. Technically, in its arrangement of material and its lightning editing, it has no better. From the newsreel to " The True Glory " is the advance from the newspaper paragraph to the considered recording of history.

I have spoken so far only of the non-fiction film, strictly speaking: of the documentary and the film of recorded fact. I have dwelt on this aspect of the British war-time cinema because the development of the non-fiction film has been significant, as we shall see, in more ways than one. But ultimately it is on the quality of its entertainment films that the prestige of a national cinema must rest. We judge a country's literature not by its text-books, not even by its histories, but rather by its imaginative works, by its poetry, its drama, its novels. So with the cinema: however marked the element of imagination in a documentary film, it is to the essentially creative work that we turn for the full judgment of value. When we think of the grandeur of the Russian cinema, it is of " Potemkin ", " Storm Over Asia ", " The End of St. Petersburg " that we think. The French cinema, so much savoured and admired in England, owes its reputation to such creative artists in fiction as René Clair, Duvivier, Renoir, Marcel Carné; just as what is truly great in the American cinema is owed to a D. W. Griffith, a Lewis Milestone, a John Ford. Like patriotism, social conscience is not enough: even truth is not enough for those who regard the film, not as a craft, but as an art. The war has not produced films (with one exception) of the first magnitude in the English cinema: it has not produced a " Grapes of Wrath " or an " All Quiet on the Western Front ". But it has set the English film on the path in which masterpieces may be created; it has established precisely what was lacking in the English cinema before 1940, a traditional English style.

In the last few months before the outbreak of war, a sense of expectancy and danger was already manifested in an output of conventional spy films and thrillers. "The Spy in Black", "Q Planes", "The Four Just Men"—both the moderate and the talented directors turned their hands to the topical potboiler. The type was naturally enough carried over into the first years of the war. Carol Reed directed a light-hearted tale of British agents in Nazi Germany, "Night Train to Munich". Anthony Asquith directed a neat little fable about resistance inside Germany, "Freedom Radio". Leslie Howard, star of the British film "Pygmalion" and later of the fabulous four-hour American film "Gone with the Wind", appeared as an academic knight-errant in a tale of rescue from a concentration camp, "Pimpernel Smith". A young and little known director, Thorold Dickinson, made a neat version of a psychological thriller, "Gaslight". Michael Powell, whose work in collaboration with Emeric Pressburger was soon to make him one of the best known of English directors, turned out a brilliant espionage squib, "Contraband", a film in which wide use was made of the London background of black-out and civil defence. Parallel with these early fantasias on adventure and the war theme, a number of fiction films, serious or flippant, wholly unconnected with the war, were presented. Gabriel Pascal, producer of "Pygmalion", directed as well as produced a film of another play by Bernard Shaw, "Major Barbara". Pascal, a flamboyant character with the talents of the impresario born, spent the last year or so of the war on yet another Shaw production: "Caesar and Cleopatra", made in Technicolor with a maximum of publicity. For this production no expense was spared: dusky performers were transported to England from every corner of the Empire and Commonwealth: and a camel, joining in the spirit of the thing, contributed to the general ballyhoo by biting the director. But in 1941, when "Major Barbara" was shown, these hilarious extravaganzas were not possible; and though the film showed much talent its theme was too perversely Shavian to endear itself to war-time audiences.

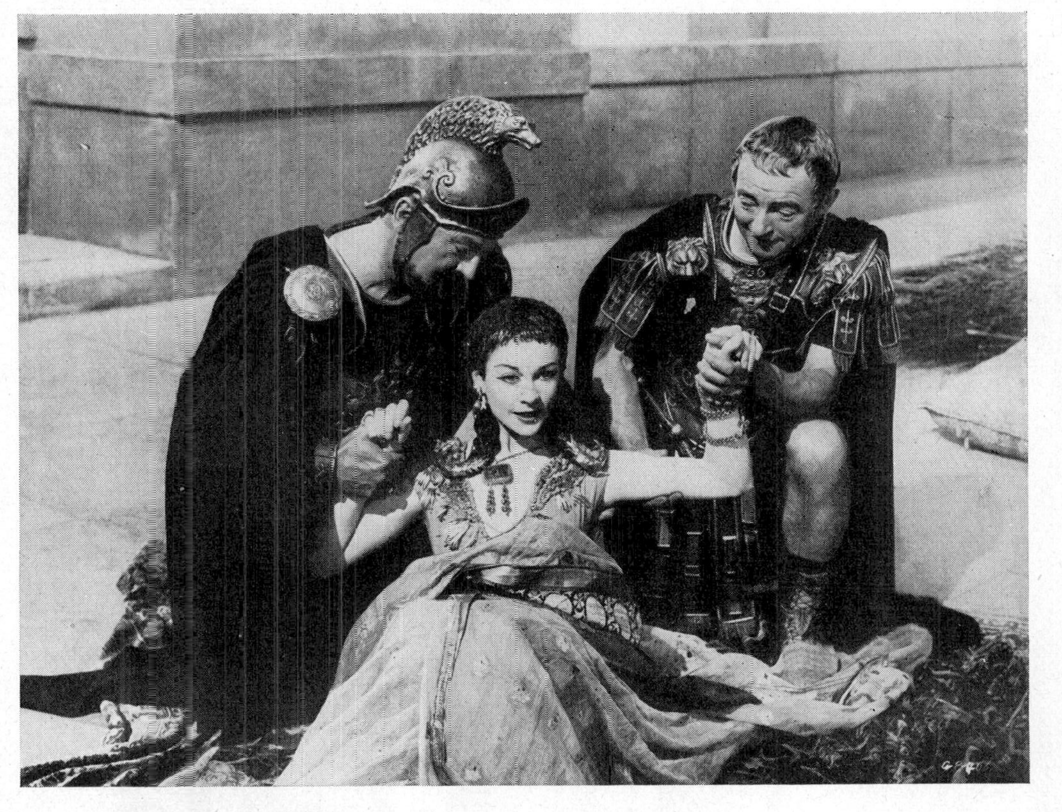

Basil Sydney, Vivien Leigh and Claude Rains in the film of Bernard Shaw's play "Caesar and Cleopatra"

From " San Demetrio, London ", directed by Charles Frend

From " Fires Were Started ", directed by Humphrey Jennings

David Niven in " The Way Ahead "

John Mills and Stewart Granger in " Waterloo Road "

Sybilla Binder and Lilli Palmer in the Boulting Brothers' production of "Thunder Rock"

Less ambitious, but far more clear-cut in its essential implications, was John Baxter's film " Love on the Dole ", from Walter Greenwood's bitter play about poverty and unemployment in the years between the wars. " Love on the Dole " was a brave film to show in the black years of the war: it savagely attacked a social and economic structure which wasted human lives in idleness and poverty, and its picture of the slump in a Lancashire factory town held no flattery for the British. Yet those who most bitterly attacked the conditions it showed could not but praise the public honesty which permitted the showing. And for its broad human playing as well as for its handling of a tragic subject, John Baxter's film remains in the mind.

In a greatly reduced output of entertainment films, one or two pieces by skilled hands stand out for their direction. Carol Reed, for instance, made, as well as his lighter pieces, a serious story of life among the North Country coal-miners, " The Stars Look Down ", from the novel by A. J. Cronin (1940). In the year following, his version of H. G. Wells's novel " Kipps " was shown: a period piece distinguished by its feeling for the background of lower class and snob life in the 'nineties, and for its many touches of pictorial wit. Anthony Asquith, again, was responsible, in 1941, for a film of a current play, " Quiet Wedding ", a comedy of manners with a setting of easy, well-to-do life in a country house. Technically these films had their points: some of them had good character acting, most showed an attention to the telling detail of background. But there was little here indicative of a new orientation in the British cinema: nothing to reflect the spiritual and emotional changes which the British people were undergoing at the time.

In 1940 two films appeared, modestly enough, made by a young director who afterwards lost his life in the war. Pen Tennyson, great-grandson of the Victorian poet, Lord Tennyson. The first, " The Proud Valley ", was a simple story of the valleys where, in their bleak huddled villages, the Welsh miners lead a life apart. The film had many technical weaknesses; some of its acting was stagy, the last reel in particular limped, since to fit the changing events of war a new end to the story had been devised. But two things kept the piece fresh in the mind: the voice of Paul Robeson, the famous American Negro bass, who played the part of an alien miner, and a curious quality of sincerity and truth in the communication of regional feeling. Some sense of the remoteness of the South Wales valleys with their slag-heaps and their bare rounded hills emerged from the narrative; here for once was some shadow of the reality of British life. The film was followed a few months later by a second Tennyson picture, " Convoy ". Here again was an uncertain piece of work with, this time, a trivial love story. But the background—the work of an Atlantic merchant convoy—was solidly based on experience; and the film included a number of shots of actual convoy operations.

Possibly neither piece would stand the test of time. The fact remains that here, in these two modest productions, were the germs of a new movement in the British cinema: the movement towards concentration on the native subject, the movement towards documentary truth in the entertainment film. The war both encouraged a new seriousness of approach by British producers and directors, and drove them to look nearer home than before in their themes. But this, naturally enough, did not happen all at once. I have said that the fall of France left Britain for the time being isolated. But while the British were still fighting a solitary battle—solitary, that is, except for the great fight of the Greeks in the Pindus Gorges and on the Albanian heights—they looked eagerly to Europe for the spirit of resistance which they knew must be stirring there. From the Continent across the Channel, travellers came back with stories beyond the invention of men; a dark curtain of secrecy had been lowered, but the British knew that beyond it a great war of sacrifice and desperation was being fought. It is easy enough to dismiss as fairy tales the series of adventure films about Occupied Europe which were made in British studios and, later, in Hollywood. Many of them, certainly, were made without knowledge or imaginative understanding of the ordeal of the European peoples. But at least some of them were an attempt at understanding. And, when all is said and done, the British contribution to the series is not negligible.

One of the earliest was made by the team of Powell and Pressburger, mentioned earlier: it was called " One of Our Aircraft is

Missing" and it told a story, boyish in spirit, perhaps, but handled with a sharp feeling for the cinema medium, of the adventures of an air crew forced to bale out in Occupied Holland. The British like to think of themselves as a people accepting danger ironically; and this side of the British character it was which coloured the film. An actor, a business man, a mechanic, a professional football player—the airmen belong to widely varying social classes. But in a tight corner they act as one man: for already, even in so light-hearted a narrative as "One of Our Aircraft is Missing", the democratic feeling of community, of men with equal rights and responsibilities, is present. As a sketch of British character, the film is, of course, superficial; as a sketch of Dutch character, trivial; but in its presentation of Dutch ingenuity in resistance, of Dutch readiness to run the risk of danger in helping the fliers to escape, it does its work honourably. And throughout the series of resistance films, the Occupied Europe cycle, as they might be called, this same emphasis on the courage and self-sacrifice of the European peoples may be observed. France, Norway, Belgium, Yugoslavia, Czechoslovakia—one after the other the Nazi-occupied countries afforded the scene for some film of adventure. Some of these pieces were frankly bad (though less bad than the analogous Hollywood series), but at least all had the merit of recognising the great contribution of the resistance movement in Europe. And occasionally something with human solidity emerged: for instance, "The Foreman Went to France", shown early in 1942. The film was directed by a newcomer, Charles Frend, with Cavalcanti as producer: perhaps something of Cavalcanti's documentary experience permeated the story: it was at any rate skilfully compounded of adventure and hard fact. Based on a story by the English writer, J. B. Priestley, it reconstructed the actual experience of an English foreman who, when the fall of France seemed imminent, crossed the Channel to recover valuable secret equipment and brought it back despite the Nazi invasion, the blocked roads, the machine-gunning and the choked Channel ports. The film had no great names in its cast. But the truth of its background and its sympathetic handling of the French catastrophe won it an honourable place among the British films of the early war period.

Interesting work, in this first part of the war, sometimes came from unexpected sources. There was, for instance, the case of "Next of Kin", a film originally intended for the fighting forces, but proving, in its making, so lively and entertaining a job that in the end it was released to the general public. "Next of Kin" was in essence a warning: a warning of the importance of secrecy in the planning of an operation. A landing on enemy-held territory is prepared: the troops are trained in isolation, the ground is reconnoitred, the naval support is ready. But from a multiplicity of tiny hints, a word dropped here, a document carelessly handled there, enemy agents deduce the plan: they are ready for the assault, and the story ends with a British radio announcement of the completed operation: "the next of kin", it says laconically in the accepted phrase, "have been informed". The virtue of the film lay partly, of course, in the singular ingenuity of its plot. But there was something else: there was the native truth of its characterisation and setting. British audiences enjoyed what has been described as one of the keenest pleasures, the pleasure of recognition: they saw themselves, their neighbours, their own shores.

A few months later a film appeared which heightened that pleasure to an extraordinary degree, which took the commonplace, the touching everyday material of life, and irradiated it with emotional sympathy.

Noel Coward, the brilliant and irreverent English playwright of the years between the wars, had been regarded in England and America as a man purely of the theatre. Elegant, cynical, he lived and breathed theatre: high comedy and drama, revue and musical romance, he wrote them all: he wrote the words, he wrote the music, he acted in the plays and the sketches. But the cinema, it seemed, lay outside his province; he had once acted in an American film ("The Scoundrel") but no more. In 1942 Coward appeared suddenly as a man of the cinema. "In Which We Serve", a story of the life of a British destroyer and her crew, was written, produced and directed by Coward: Coward wrote the music and played the part of the destroyer's captain. The film astonished a public accustomed to look on the author as the perpetual play-boy. The framework of the film was simple enough. A destroyer is sunk off

Crete; a party of her crew struggle towards a raft; as each man feels the water closing above his head, or fights for life under enemy machine-gunning, fragments of the past circle, float and steady in his mind. Thus we see, linked by the shared experience of the ship and the sea, the lives of the survivors at their most significant moments: the captain taking over his command, a raw young sailor yielding to panic in a naval engagement, a petty officer spending Christmas at home with his family. For the loose web of narrative holds land as well as sea: the rescue of survivors from Dunkirk, a wedding, an air raid. One of the most moving passages in this moving film shows three women, waiting in their house in the great port of Plymouth, listening for the scream of the bombs; with a rare understanding of human behaviour in extreme peril, Coward has made the women complain a little, scold, talk of trivialities.

The emotional impact of " In Which We Serve " was immense. The experiences of civilian and fighting men were presented as essentially one, bound together by the ties of human love and devotion; nobody but felt he had a stake in this drama. But if we look at the film with a detached and critical eye we must recognise the technical skill, the command of the medium which has gone to its making. The authority with which the complex strands of the narrative are handled, the mastery of simple unemphatic dialogue, the easy unobtrusive use of camera angle and movement —all are here. And the acting was pretty near faultless. Not all critics have praised Coward's own performance as the captain; there is, perhaps, a trace of self-satisfaction in it. Yet in the emotional climaxes of the film—the colloquy between captain and dying sailor, the last good-bye between captain and crew—there is no self consciousness. The film brought prestige also to many players not, till then, recognised as first-rank film performers. To Celia Johnson, for example, a polished stage actress, who now brought an easy technique to the part of the captain's wife; to John Mills, everlastingly English as the naval rating; to Bernard Miles as the petty officer and to Richard Attenborough as the frightened boy. Coward, during the rest of the war, directed no more films, though he was the author of more than one. But

"In Which We Serve" had set a new standard in the English cinema.

There is nothing experimental, certainly nothing revolutionary, in the style of "In Which We Serve". What makes it historically important in the British cinema is its use of two significant motives: documentary background and the native theme. The film opens with a purely documentary sequence presenting the building of a warship; and throughout the story is underpinned, as it were, by fact, the fact of the sailor's life. But even more important at this stage was the emphasis on a subject germane to the experience of every man, woman and child in the audience. I have said that before the war the British cinema had no tradition. One might go further and say it had no subject. Looking back at the history of the cinema in Europe and America, one detects, beneath the superficial variety of themes, something which might be called a national theme. The French, a people with a deep and tender feeling for the under-side of life, the shadowed pavement of the street, the human unfortunate, have made their best films on the theme of undisciplined life. Renoir, Carné, Duvivier, René Clair, have shown us the crook, the vagabond, rather than the established citizen, the raffish boarding-house rather than the *bourgeois* home; the picture has been translated into a kind of poetic realism which found beauty in the smoky confusion of the railway viaduct, the quayside, the murky back-street. In the great days of the Russian cinema, the theme was revolution, the protagonists were the infantryman in the trenches, the half-starved sailor, the suffering worker in farm and factory; and once more a savagely dramatic handling of pictorial values translated the realistic scene into poetry. The American cinema at its best, on the other hand, has dealt with the brilliant surface of life. The poetic overtones of D. W. Griffith's great films were lost in the work of his successors: and the American cinema became a representation, fast-moving, sometimes ironic, always realistic, of the face of America: the face of the crowded city, the face of the enormous landscape. Always, one sees, the concentration on native material. It is when the French producers, or the Russian, or the American, venture outside their own national experience, that they most obviously fail.

This is not simply because the cinema, however poetically handled, must rely on a basis of realism. Superficially realism can be acquired; an Englishman can learn the factual background of life in, say, New York. It is a thousand times more difficult for him to acquire the rhythm and cadence of American life. The film, in its natural dependence on material native to producers and directors, does not differ from the other arts: Tolstoy uses his immense genius on Russian subjects, the great English novelist, Dickens, builds up his superb tragi-comic picture of life from the London and the England he knows.

This concentration on inherited and contemporary experience was almost completely lacking in the British cinema of the 'twenties and 'thirties. Subjects were to hand; for Britain in its small compass holds an infinite variety of ways of life, of types, from the factory-worker in the Northern and industrial towns to the fisherman of the Scottish coasts, from the shepherd of the South Downs to the steel-worker, the coal-miner, the railwayman, the shipbuilder. It took a war to compel the British to look at themselves and find themselves interesting. This did not mean, as I hope I have made clear, anything resembling isolationism. The British remained indefatigably curious about the outside world from which war had cut them off. But the circumstances of war, the total effort of the country, narrowed the physical circle in which the creative imagination could work; intent on the business of daily survival, the national conscience began to dwell more than ever before on its local problems. Noel Coward in " In Which We Serve " took a handful of typically British men and women and made from their stories, ordinary enough in themselves, a distillation of national character. The films of the same period, or of the years which followed, may have been uneven and faltering. But at least they showed a movement towards a national subject, in the sense in which I have just used the phrase.

Coward's film spoke for the Navy, to some effect, for tough though the British sailor holds himself, admirals and ratings alike were observed in tears at its performance. It was not until two years later that a film was made to speak in like terms for the British Army. In 1944 Carol Reed's " The Way Ahead " was presented:

a film with an emphatically documentary technique, and, again, with this same natural understanding of British character. Briefly, it was the story of a British army unit composed of men drawn, unwillingly enough, from a great variety of classes and callings. The Briton is a reluctant soldier; he hates war, he hates the disruption of his life, however humdrum; he hates discipline, though having once accepted it, he is its servant. " The Way Ahead " (whose script, by the way, was written in collaboration by Peter Ustinov and a British writer of thrillers, Eric Ambler) showed us the gradual transformation of a bunch of individualists into an integrated, disciplined military unit. Training, embarkation, the troopship torpedoed on the way to North Africa, the landing and the long period of waiting for action—here was the experience of thousands of British soldiers. What made the narrative significant was its sympathetic yet ironic portrayal of character and the emergence of an idea, the idea of readiness for sacrifice; when the last shot fades from the screen, the men we have come to know are moving forward into battle: there, untried, unknown, is the way ahead.

This mingling of documentary technique and native character marks many British war films. For example, " Nine Men ", a fictitious episode from the Libyan Campaign, told the story of a British patrol lost in the desert and fighting off a massive enemy attack; the director, Harry Watt, famous for his handling of " Target for Tonight ", used no well-known actors, but relied rather on realism of dialogue and setting. Leslie Howard (who later was to lose his life when the passenger plane in which he was travelling was shot down by the Nazis) threw himself into production as well as acting. Of his two last films, one, " The First of the Few ", was a reconstruction of the life and work of R. J. Mitchell, designer of the Spitfire (the fighter plane which won the Battle of Britain). In the other, " The Gentle Sex ", Howard did not himself appear, but spoke the commentary which linked the narrative; this was a film about the work of recruits to the A.T.S., the Auxiliary Territorial Service, in which women acted not merely as clerks or telephonists, but also as despatch riders and anti-aircraft gunners.

One or two films devoted to the part played by women in the

war are worth remembering. " The Lamp Still Burns " brought a critical sympathy to bear on the life of a hospital nurse, still hedged in by regulations often outdated. And " Millions Like Us " portrayed with delicate sensibility the life of the woman munitions worker: in this case a girl eager to serve in the Forces but, as a conscript, drafted instead to the necessary work of armaments supply. " Millions Like Us " was a first essay in direction by two men of the cinema who had formerly worked only as script-writers: Frank Launder and Sidney Gilliat. In British studios, as in American and French studios, the importance of the script-writer has not always been recognised. And in Britain, at any rate, one of the interesting developments has been the emergence of a school of writers for the film, conscious of their own power and bent on its acknowledgment. Launder and Gilliat had for some time worked as a team; their script for Hitchcock's pre-war thriller " The Lady Vanishes " was a model of witty writing for the screen. Now they decided to try directing their own scripts, at first jointly, later individually; and " Millions Like Us " betrayed, in its natural dialogue and grasp of situation, an unusual awareness of the medium. I recall, for example, the tiny scene in which a girl is called from her work in the factory to receive the news that her husband, a young airman, has been killed. The scene is presented in hints rather than direct representation; the door of the Supervisor's room is left half open, a figure rushes out calling for a glass of water, and, without a word said, the audience knows that the girl has understood.

Not all the best talent, of course, took readily to the documentary style which, for a time, prevailed in almost every film. Anthony Asquith, for example, a director with a pretty pictorial wit and a strong poetic feeling, sometimes gave the impression that he was working against the grain ; his story of life in a submarine, " We Dive at Dawn ", efficient though it was in a cold way, lacked the warmth of life. But with a later film, " The Way to the Stars " (1945), he succeeded admirably in capturing the emotion trembling beneath the laconic phrase, the controlled emotion. " The Way to the Stars " was a film about Anglo-American co-operation in air warfare: its scene, an English airfield from the

Battle of Britain to the early raids by flying fortresses, its characters the dwindling band of experienced British pilots, and the American newcomers, who slowly learn to understand the British habit of understatement. Beautifully played by John Mills, Michael Redgrave and Rosamund John, the film holds, for anyone who has lived through the years of air battle over England, an incomparable quality of regret for the massacre of youth.

Yet there is no denying that a natural talent is at its best when working in its own manner, and to my mind Asquith's abilities were better shown in his satirical comedy, " The Demi-Paradise " (1943), the story of a Soviet engineer sent before the Nazi invasion of Russia to place an order in England. This film drew a picture, ironic and yet at the same time affectionate, of English foibles. The visitor encounters all the surface idiosyncrasies of a reserved people: the unwelcoming landlady, the silent railway travellers, the apparent casualness and coldness and suspicion of the average Englishman towards a foreigner. The Russian is chilled and discouraged until, with the entry of his country into the war against Germany, the genuine warmth and friendliness underlying British reserve come into play. " The Demi-Paradise " had innumerable touches of pictorial satire: for example, the parody of the village pageant, got up, in the English way, in aid of charity, with the well-meaning assistance of the whole community from local squire to local labourer. The film is remarkable too for the beautiful performance of Sir Laurence Olivier as the bewildered Russian, a performance which put him for the first time in the top flight of British film actors. Olivier began his career as a stage actor in England, then worked for some time in Hollywood, achieving there a considerable success. During the war he and his wife, Vivien Leigh, came back to their own country, preferring to work in the service of England. In the last few years both have won considerable fame on the London stage. Olivier has done more; his performances in English classical drama with the famous repertory company known as the Old Vic have given him a position almost without rival; at last the English feel that they have a great contemporary tragedian. But stage work did not exclude the cinema; Vivien Leigh was to play Cleopatra in Pascal's " Caesar and Cleopatra ", and

Olivier produced, directed and played the name part in the superb Technicolor film of Shakespeare's historical play, " Henry V ".

The satirical manner of " The Demi-Paradise " was reflected in one or two other comedies of character in 1944 and 1945: for instance, in " Tawny Pipit ", a satire on the Englishman's passion for natural history, made by another actor turned director, Bernard Miles (the petty officer of " In Which We Serve "). " Tawny Pipit " was a fable of the appearance in an English village of a pair of rare migrant birds; lest the visitors should be disturbed, military manœuvres in the neighbourhood are held up and the entire local population conspires to keep off or, in the last resort kidnap, inquisitive ornithologists. A satire on English country life was to be found also in " Don't Take it to Heart ", made by yet another script-writer turned director, Jeffrey Dell. Here the joke was against the decaying traditions of aristocratic life, against the medieval manor with its antiquated heating system, its long corridors, its whole outworn system of life—and against the impoverished gentry, only too ready to renounce the inconvenience of keeping up appearances. The other side of the country picture was shown in Powell and Pressburger's " A Canterbury Tale ", a film remarkable for its visual beauty, yet failing, as many British films have failed, through want of a strong and convincing plot. Shots of the pacific English countryside with its rich woods and fields and the immemorial round of labour marked the new appreciation in English studios of the value and interest of the native scene. English urban life, on the other hand, was the setting of Sidney Gilliat's " Waterloo Road ", a beautifully composed story of an English soldier, absent without leave because some busy-body has told him that his wife is " carrying on ", in the colloquial phrase, with one of the profiteers of London's underworld. The film made use of two successful and popular players, John Mills and Stewart Granger. Excellent performances from both did not, however, obscure the fact that the real quality of the film lay in its sympathetic yet realistic handling of the lower strata of English city life; here once more was the reunion of the native theme with the factual documentary background.

I have said that Noel Coward, after " In Which We Serve ",

directed no more films during the war. But his creative impulse continued to play its part in the British cinema. In 1944 his play of London suburban life, " This Happy Breed " (a title taken from John of Gaunt's speech in Shakespeare's *Richard II*), was presented as a film. It was directed by an able young technician, David Lean, and played by, among others, John Mills, Celia Johnson and Robert Newton. For the first time in the British cinema an attempt was made to present a realistic subject in Technicolor; for this tale of a middle-class family living obscurely, yet in its own way passionately, through the years between the wars, is nothing if not realistic. Happy touches of character and a delicate play of sensibility illuminate the story. Yet to my mind Coward does not achieve here the precise statement of British character of " In Which We Serve ". The approach is more detached; look, the film seems to be saying, look at these unassuming people, see of what heroic metal they are framed! There is even a touch of patronage now and then; Coward is here not speaking with his characters, but about them. A film in the playwright's pre-war cynical manner, " Blithe Spirit " (the play ran for five years on the London stage), was perhaps more of a piece; here, in this sketch of frivolous, heartless society, Coward identifies himself with his characters. The film, directed again by David Lean, is a brilliant joke on the theme, not generally regarded as a fit subject for laughter, of death and spiritualism. A writer, comfortably jogging along with his second wife, is suddenly visited by the ghostly figure of his first wife; visible to him only, she sits in his drawing-room, occupies his study, accompanies him when he drives his car into town. Finally she engineers the early demise of his second wife; and now this double widower is haunted by two figures, united at least in their desire to annoy. This film also was made in Technicolor; the capabilities of the camera to present the supernatural were used but not over-used; witty dialogue and pictorial joke played each its part in the sophisticated jest. The British cinema had asserted its capacity for smooth high comedy.

Two other films by the Powell-Pressburger team should not be passed over. The first, " 49th Parallel ", was among the earliest British war films; it appeared in 1941, almost at the beginning of the anti-Nazi series. Its value depends partly on the quality of its acting and direction, partly on its unfamiliar setting. Here, for once, was a film which used as its background part of the British Commonwealth; to be exact, the Dominion of Canada. A German submarine crew are wrecked in the Hudson Estuary; in a bold attempt at escape they try to cross Canada and make their way into the United States of America, at that time still neutral. By treachery and murder the captain and a dwindling band of the crew cross city and plain, only to be outmanœuvred at the last. There were critics who saw in the film something like glorification of Nazi resolution and enterprise; indeed there were moments in the story when, however brutal the behaviour of the fugitives, British sympathies were involved on behalf of the hunted as against the hunter. Yet basically the film was an argument against the ethics of power and force; everywhere the Nazis go they are met by the unity of men prepared for sacrifice and suffering in defence of peace and justice. And "49th Parallel" presented a superb picture of the face of Canada: a country of vast spaces, of woods and lakes and rich cornlands, inhabited by the infinite variety of mankind.

The second Powell-Pressburger film was an interesting experiment in social history and the development of a point of view: it was called "The Life and Death of Colonel Blimp". Blimp was originally a creation of the British cartoonist, David Low: an emblem of reaction and the die-hard, represented always as a stout old gentleman with walrus moustaches. In the film, Blimp's development is seen from his beginnings in youth and enthusiasm, through romantic disappointment, to his end as a hide-bound stickler for form, a mind incapable of understanding the issues at stake and the new desperate spirit of modern warfare. Yet it is not an unsympathetic portrait The old man is spiritually rigid only because he has been brought up in an honourable tradition and believes in war as an occupation for a gentleman. It is to the film's credit, perhaps, that the issues are not cut-and-dried; the cinema is accused often enough of an over-simplification of characters and morals, and here is an attempt at presenting two sides of the case. Technically the film was uneven, but contained passages which can be described only as masterly: the treatment, for example, of the duel, fought in the early part of the film between Blimp and a young German, is cinema at its best.

Once or twice during the war years a film appeared in the British studios which stood by itself, which had no model and no successor. Such is " Thunder Rock ", a film, with a supernatural background, from an American stage play; it was made by two brothers, Roy Boulting, distinguished for his work in " Desert Victory " and " Burma Victory ", and his brother John, who, late in the war, directed a sensitive study in the semi-documentary *genre*, " Journey Together ". " Thunder Rock " was the story of the conversion of an escapist, a man disgusted by the evidence of human blindness to the imminent catastrophe of war, who takes refuge in solitude on a lighthouse rock. But his solitude is not absolute. Years before, a ship bringing refugees from the restless Europe of the nineteenth century had foundered on this very rock; the spirits of the drowned haunt him with their memories of the evils from which they fled; and at the last he realises that, had they only waited and resisted, they would have seen the end of their difficulties. The moral is thus one of action as against yielding, patience as against flight; and if the central character lacks something in solidity, the weakness is in the original idea, not in the film portrait. Certainly not in the acting; for " Thunder Rock " gave a chance to a distinguished young stage and screen actor, Michael Redgrave (seen also in " The Way to the Stars "), which he did not fail to seize.

The supernatural element in this film was bred of imagination, not fact; the spirits who point the escapist to his duty live in his own imagination. Two later films seem to give promise of a talent for the handling of the traditional ghost story. The first, " The Half-Way House " (1944), a story of a country inn destroyed by bombing but materialising on the anniversary of its destruction, made good use of the background of British landscape. The second, " Dead of Night " (1945), marked, it seems to me, a new stage in film ghost stories. To begin with, much of its material was specially written for the screen, with a grasp of pictorial narrative rare in Britain or anywhere else. Secondly, the whole film ends on a note of uncertainty which beautifully echoes the true terror of the supernatural; there are no facile explanations, only the appalling mystery of the irrational, the undeserved. " Dead of Night ", consisting as it did of a group of ghost stories enclosed within the frame-work of a ghost story, was unequal in quality. But its two most successful episodes, a tale of a haunted mirror, beautifully conceived in visual terms, and a dreadful little sketch of a ventriloquist possessed by his dummy, acted by Michael Redgrave and directed by Cavalcanti, are technically almost irreproachable.

The impetus of war gave a new concentration and a new urgency to the themes and the treatment of British films. " Dead of Night " and a small group of other fiction films, divorced from the background of war, show that the new talents released between 1940 and 1945 did not depend for their success on the sensation of national crisis. But there were, of course, many inferior films, films on trivial conventional themes trivially handled. A group of cheaply romantic costume pieces, for example, seem to me undeserving of the popular success they have won; and the talent or personality of such players as James Mason, Stewart Granger and Phyllis Calvert cannot disguise the novelettish feeling of these pieces. Even the authority of Anthony Asquith, who directed one of them, " Fanny by Gaslight " (1944), could not, with all his feeling for period decoration, convert this story of nineteenth-century raffish London life into anything but a romance for schoolgirls.

Against these, and rising above the common run of moderate or even distinguished films, we can set a few achievements remarkable by any standard. I have already mentioned Sir Laurence Olivier's production of Shakespeare's " Henry V ". The wisdom of presenting the great classics of literature on the screen has long been debated, and there is no denying that in general, where a masterpiece is translated into another medium, there is a sad diminution of genius. Shakespeare in particular had suffered; the conflict between a pictorial medium and an original depending on verbal mastery had never been resolved; in all the earlier Shakespeare films the poetry had been obscured by visual images ranging from the pretty to the vulgar. It was therefore with a shock of surprise and delight that the spectator found in "Henry V" the perfect marriage of visual and verbal poetry. The text with its great clarion speeches was left, with a few cuts, untouched; to it the film added a superb pictorial narrative, supplementing but not overpowering Shakespeare's narrative. The transition from stage to screen was most subtly handled; opening with a stage production of the play as it might have been given in Shakespeare's own time at the old Elizabethan Globe Theatre, the action moved by barely perceptible stages into the open fields of realism, into the battle of Agincourt, the cavalry charge, the rout of the French knights. Stylised settings based on French paintings of the period smoothed the transition, so that when the scene changed to real fields, real woods, the audience accepted without question. The battle itself, with the great line of cavalry moving in a measured walk, a trot, a canter and at last a wild gallop, trumpets blowing and pennants flying, had an excitement and a rhythm comparable only to the battle scenes in Eisenstein's "Alexander Nevsky"; with this difference, that in the British film the use of colour, bold and imaginative, enormously heightened the dramatic tension. Acting in the finest traditions of the British stage gave body to the picture; and as the young King, Sir Laurence Olivier created something almost unknown in the cinema: the heroic *poetic* figure.

Thus colour, faltering though it must still be in the present stages of technical command, comes at last into its own in the imaginative and dramatic cinema. Into its own, too, in the realistic cinema: for example, in the British Council's magnificently pictorial documentary, "Steel". I have already mentioned the beautiful semi-documentary war film, "Western Approaches", the story, played by non-professional actors, of a merchantman torpedoed in mid-Atlantic. In "Western Approaches" for the first time colour was used to intensify sober dramatic truth; lapses in realism there were, but in the shots of the spumy Atlantic, the ship's boat drifting in the immense solitude, the pale dawn breaking or the midday brilliance, there was something as yet unknown in cinema narrative. Let me emphasise once more the importance of the new semi-documentary *genre* to which belong "Western Approaches", and such black-and-white films as Boulting's "Journey

From " Love on the Dole ", directed by John Baxter

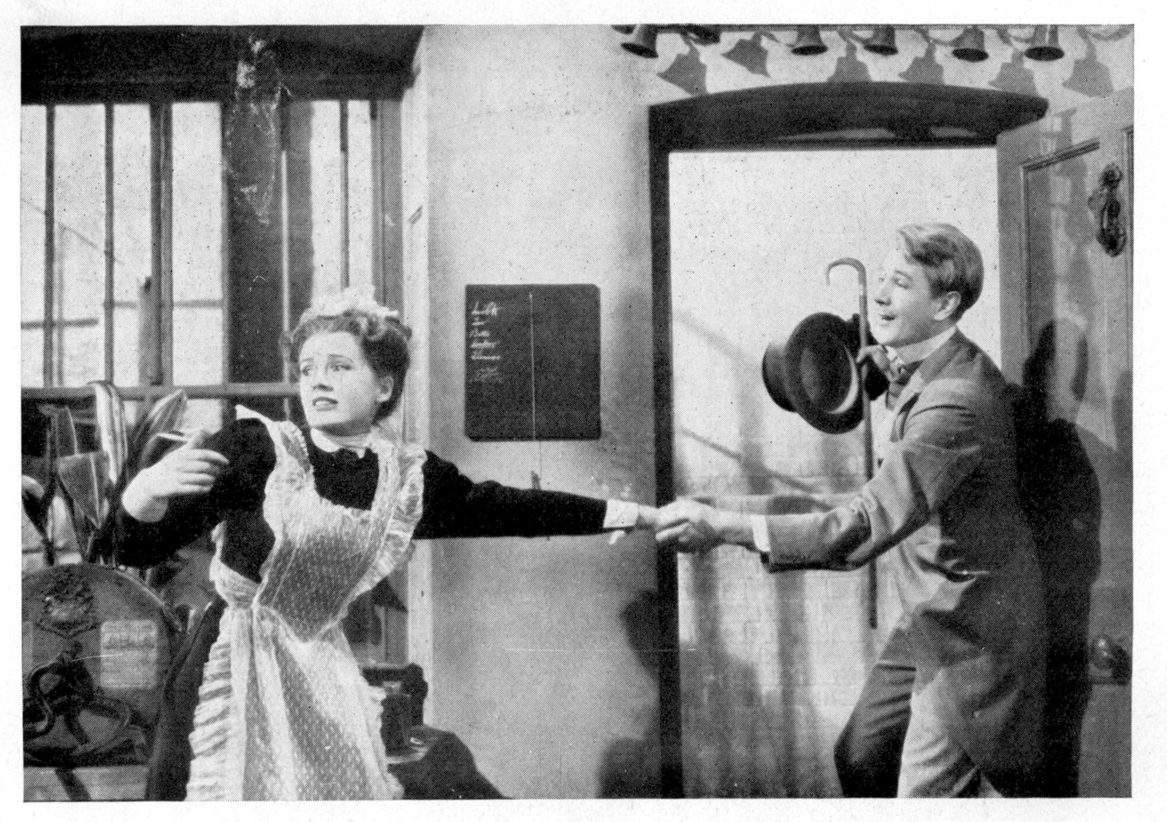

Phyllis Calvert and Michael Redgrave in the film of H. G. Wells's novel " Kipps "

Michael Redgrave in a sequence, directed by Cavalcanti, from " Dead of Night "

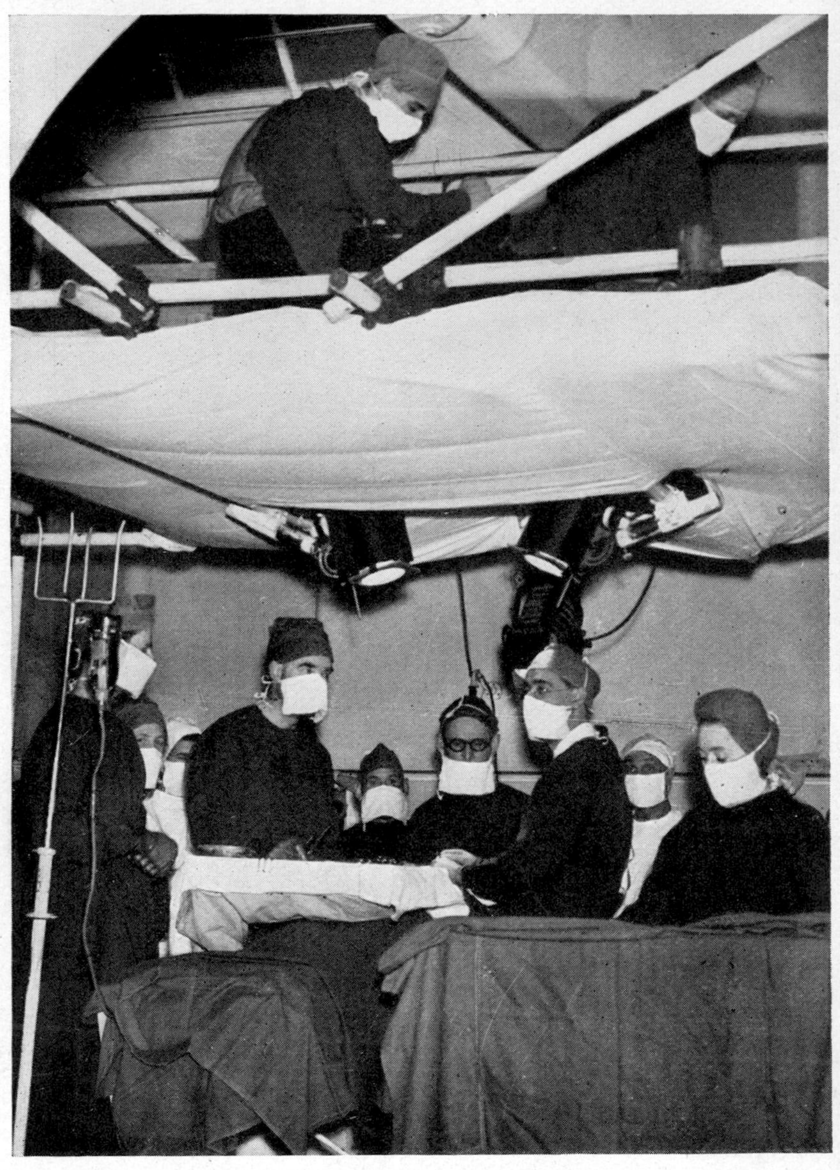

In a London hospital during the making of the British Council's medical film, " Surgery in Chest Diseases "
Below, the surgeon ready to operate ; *Above*, the camera crew

Together" (a story of the training of air cadets), Harry Watt's "Target for Tonight", Charles Frend's "San Demetrio, London" (a reconstruction of the true story of a British tanker, set on fire by a German raider, abandoned, and re-boarded by sixteen of her crew, who brought her without chart, without wireless, compass or bridge, safe home to a Scottish port). The film in its present stage of development is a realistic medium. But it is capable, as I have said, of poetic realism; and, in the hands of some of the young documentary producers and directors, of a new kind of poetic impressionism. Humphrey Jennings, director of the semi-documentary "Fires Were Started", and of "The Silent Village" (a reconstruction, in terms of a Welsh mining village, of the story of the Nazi massacre of Lidice) made, for instance, a bold experiment with sight and sound in "Listen to Britain", a short film presenting war-time Britain through her everyday voices—the factory whistle, the tramp of marching soldiers, the country song of birds, the hum of London crowds. And, in an age when State control is accused of failure in imaginativeness and aesthetic sense, it should not be forgotten that under British Government sponsorship "Our Country" was produced—a poetic record of the face of Britain, marrying exquisitely composed pictures of city and farm, mountain and highway, with an impressionistic verse commentary.

All such experiments do not succeed; and I, for one, much as I admired the pictorial qualities of "Our Country" and the lively imagery of its verse, did not feel that together verbal and visual image created an integrated whole. But the creative impulse was there: the creative impulse which, through six years of war, has kept the British cinema alive. New talents have emerged and old talents come to maturity in these years of crisis. New audiences too have come into being. For while, in the cinemas of city and town, serving men and women and civilians crowded for the week's fiction, whether British or American, a great new public was being created by what is known in Britain as the non-theatrical movement, that is to say, the showing of films in factories, in village halls, in Women's Institutes up and down the country. Mobile projectors travelled the length of Britain, presenting to these new audiences shows of documentary and instructional films, films often specially designed for the purpose. Some idea of the magnitude of this operation may be gathered from the fact that between August 1943 and August 1944, eleven and a half million people were entertained by the non-theatrical programmes of the Ministry of Information. Of these millions, not all were easy customers. I remember, for instance, visiting a munitions factory in South Wales in the summer of 1941; at the lunch hour, women workers in their hundreds clattered from the sheds into the canteen room where, while they ate their sandwiches and drank their strong tea, documentary films about air training in Canada and the British Army health services were shown on the screen. The noise was incessant and savage; a third of the audience paid little attention to the performance, and of the rest probably the majority were tolerant rather than interested. Yet something was communicated, the effort was not vain; for as the war years continued it was found that the demand in just such factories for just such performances grew insistent. At the other end of the scale were the audiences still quite ignorant of the cinema and still fascinated by its mechanical wonders. In the evening of the day on which I had visited the factory, I was taken to a mining village, remote at the head of a valley: just such a village, perhaps, as we saw in Pen Tennyson's film. A mobile film van had arrived; the village hall was thrown open; and, at the end of the day's work, miners and their wives sat rapt and silent through a documentary record of the making of an airscrew.

The British public, always a cinema-going public, had thus become doubly so during the war years. And with the increase in numbers, a certain sharpening of public taste is to be observed. Themes which would once have been thought too serious or too controversial for the ordinary spectator are now accepted as a matter of course. The success of Rotha's " World of Plenty " is an example; here was a piece concerned with the strategy of food, with one of the most difficult and complicated of international economic problems. Yet it was welcomed by the same public which, every week, attends the farce, the musical, the banal screen fairy-tale. Something more than opportunity must be called in to explain this development of public interest. Life, perhaps, has grown more serious for the clerk, the artisan, the ordinary man and woman of Great Britain in the last decade. To the ordinary fears and ambitions of ordinary life have been added new fears and new ambitions; ambitions for a life of fresh material potentialities, fears of the total breakdown of the civilised structure of existence. The individual can no longer escape into the private circle of life; the circumstances of the new world demand of him an attention to problems outside his own work, even outside his own country. Parallel with what is, I believe, a permanent orientation towards internationalism, there is a desire for solidity and truth, even in the sphere of entertainment. We have seen how the semi-documentary film has gained a hold over British imaginations. We have seen too how even in the film of simple fiction, the demand has grown for knowledge and understanding. The British no longer demand pure fantasy in their films; they can be receptive also to the imaginative interpretation of everyday life. The serious British film has thus found an audience as well as a subject. If it preserves its newly-found standards of conception and technique, it will find not merely a national, but an international audience.

MUSIC SINCE 1939

ROLLO H. MYERS

MUSIC SINCE 1939

THIS account of musical events in Britain since the outbreak of war in 1939 surveys the varied work, in the face of almost overwhelming difficulties, of C.E.M.A., E.N.S.A., the London and provincial orchestras, the Promenade and National Gallery Concerts, the B.B.C. and the British Council, and deals with the many new works of British composers written during this period. The especial interest of the essay lies in its illustration of the great contribution which these activities made to the growth in Britain of musical appreciation, and in particular of the knowledge of the music of this country, which had been directly stimulated by the war.

Mr. Rollo Myers is well known as a writer, critic, broadcaster and lecturer on twentieth-century music. His published works include *Music in the Modern World*, which has been translated into Dutch and Swedish, and his biographies of Erik Satie and Debussy are in preparation; he has also contributed to the leading musical periodicals in Britain and abroad, and is at present editor of *The Chesterian*.

CONTENTS

ILLUSTRATIONS

MUSIC SINCE 1939

I. MUSICIANS IN BATTLE-DRESS

On the outbreak of war in September 1939 music in Britain was in a flourishing state. The London Music Festival held in May had been widely attended by visitors from all parts of the world, and was dominated by the presence of Toscanini, who had conducted a brilliantly successful series of concerts given by the B.B.C. Symphony Orchestra in the Queen's Hall. All over the country people were taking an ever-increasing interest in music; high-class concerts were attracting large audiences in all the leading towns; and the programmes broadcast by the B.B.C. were creating a new public for music in every corner of the British Isles. British composers too were by now not only established firmly in the esteem of music-lovers at home, they were receiving for the first time in foreign countries the recognition that was their due. In a word, the musical horizon in Britain was clear, and the barometer pointed unmistakably to a long period of " set fair ".

But with the dropping of the first German bombs on Poland on 1st September 1939 conditions changed over-night. A blow had been struck at the very foundations of peace, brutally interrupting that international harmony so essential for the healthy development of universal culture. In England musicians were the first to suffer. Uncertainty as to the future and fears of immediate bombing dislocated professional life in every branch. Artists had their contracts cancelled; concert-giving organisations were unable to lay their plans; and most composers found it impossible to proceed, for the time being, with work in progress. Evacuation and dispersal were the order of the day, and all this led to a suspension of musical activities, which, however regrettable, could hardly have been avoided.

Gradually, however, as the first months of the " phoney " war wore on, it became possible to take stock of the situation, and soon tentative attempts were made in various ways to get music started again and organised on a war-time footing. It must be admitted that the music programmes broadcast by the B.B.C. in the early months of the war erred on the side of timidity, preference being given to the banal and ultra-familiar, with an excessive amount of programme time devoted to the broadcasting of commercial gramophone records. It must be borne in mind, however, that the principal broadcasting orchestras and programme staffs were evacuated to their war-time bases as soon as hostilities were declared, and this naturally entailed a considerable amount of administrative readjustment. Military service also claimed a considerable percentage of orchestral personnel throughout the country; and this of course affected every branch of the musical profession, which lost to one or other of the services a number of gifted musicians of both sexes. In due course, however, many of our leading executants were drafted into specially constituted service orchestras, chief among which was the Symphony Orchestra of the Royal Air Force (Director, Wing-Commander R. P. O'Donnell), which absorbed a large percentage of our best string and wind players, and did much to keep the flag of music flying wherever service men and women were congregated in camps and training centres all over the British Isles.

C.E.M.A.

The year 1940 also saw the foundation of two institutions which played a very important part during the war years in keeping music alive and rendering it accessible to vast numbers of people, war workers of all kinds and members of the Armed Forces. These were C.E.M.A. (Council for the Encouragement of Music and the Arts) and E.N.S.A. (Entertainments National Service Association). C.E.M.A. was started in June 1940 with a financial grant from the Pilgrim Trust and from the Treasury, while E.N.S.A., which catered more especially for the entertainment of the troops, came on the scene in October of the same year. Both these bodies organised concerts in air-raid shelters, factories, canteens and rest centres throughout the worst period of the Luftwaffe's offensive against this country, and the valuable work done by singers and instrumentalists who risked their lives during the heaviest raids "to bring the comforts and solace of fine music to those who were homeless and stricken" (to quote the words of Dr. Reginald Jacques, at that time musical Director of C.E.M.A.) is beyond all praise. It can truly be said that musicians were in the front line all through the war, because not only did they carry on in England during the various bombardments, but they also went overseas under the auspices of E.N.S.A. to give concerts to the troops on every front from Alamein to Burma.

C.E.M.A. (now known as the "Arts Council of Great Britain" or "Arts Council"), under the chairmanship of the late Lord Keynes, besides organising concerts with its own artists, many of which were (and still are) regularly broadcast, also gave financial support to Symphony Orchestras and Music Clubs in the form of guarantees against loss, and acted as agent for concerts arranged by the British Council for American troops, or by the Y.M.C.A. (Young Men's Christian Association) for British Forces in their camps and training centres. It also sponsored concerts for troops given by the B.B.C. Symphony Orchestra and other leading orchestras, and one of its most successful and interesting ventures was the organising of concerts of string music given in old and historic buildings in provincial towns. In all these activities C.E.M.A. had the expert guidance and support of a Music Advisory Panel consisting of well-known musicians, composers, performers and conductors. Some idea of the work accomplished may be gained from the following figures for one year only (1944): the Hallé Orchestra of Manchester, the Liverpool Philharmonic and the London Philharmonic provided between them no less than 722 concerts to audiences totalling over a million; while the approximate amounts paid by Chamber Music Clubs associated with C.E.M.A. in fees to professional artists rose from £800 in 1941 to £7,500 in 1944.

E.N.S.A.

The work of E.N.S.A. lay chiefly in the direction of bringing entertainment to British and American troops both at home and abroad—work which entailed sacrifices on the part of artists and all concerned, faced as they were with the difficulties of war-time travel and of giving concerts under conditions which were often far from easy or agreeable. For example, eight concerts for troops and war workers in one day, ranging from the Isle of Wight to Belfast, was by no means a rare occurrence; and to these activities at home must be added the regular provision of music to our troops on all the fronts overseas and in stations in the Middle and Far East, such as Gibraltar, Malta, Cairo, Palestine, India and Burma. In 1943 a new experiment was tried in the form of a series of symphony concerts given by the B.B.C. Symphony Orchestra for men of the Army and Navy in their barracks at Aldershot and Portsmouth. The programmes of these concerts included not only classical works, such as symphonies and concertos by Mozart and Brahms, and songs by Schubert, Wolf and Grieg, but also modern compositions by Walton, Bax and Sibelius; and although many of the men were hearing this type of music for the first time, they listened with concentrated attention and expressed their appreciation in the most enthusiastic manner. Naturally not all the music provided by E.N.S.A. was up to this standard, but the experiment showed that the most unlikely audiences will appreciate good music if given the chance of hearing it.

L.P.O. Tours

Indeed, one of the most remarkable features of musical life in Britain during the war was the quite phenomenal rise in popularity of symphonic music, which was made accessible to and enjoyed by sections of the community,—soldiers, sailors, airmen, factory workers, etc.—who up till then had shown little signs of appreciating classical music—perhaps from lack of opportunities. This phenomenon was especially noticeable among the inhabitants of some of the smaller provincial towns; and when the London Philharmonic Orchestra, conducted by Sir Malcolm Sargent, made history by going on tour, in 1940, and playing to working-class audiences in a number of industrial towns in the Midlands and North of England, they were received with such enthusiasm that the small theatres and music-halls and cinemas, which often had to do duty for non-existent concert-halls, were packed to overflowing night after night. Symphonic music henceforth was accepted by the

The late Sir Henry Wood conducting one of his Promenade Concerts
at the Royal Albert Hall, London

A concert organised by C.E.M.A. in the village church at Thaxted, Essex

Queen's Hall, the first home of the " Proms ", seen through the Orchestra room, after its destruction by enemy action in 1941

Basil Cameron conducting the London Symphony Orchestra at a Promenade Concert

workers and ceased from then on to be the prerogative of a musical *élite*. The story is worth telling, for it is typical of a phenomenon (namely, a most remarkable and ever-increasing appetite for good music amongst the people of Great Britain) which seems to have been directly stimulated by the war. The orchestra's tour was not, however, carried out in conditions of comfort and security, for it had scarcely started (this was in August 1940) when the Luftwaffe's raids on Southern England began, and soon spread to towns in the North and Midlands which were to be included in the tour. And yet throughout the whole period, in spite of the dislocation of communications, travelling difficulties, and all the dangers and discomforts of concert-giving under fire, not one member of the orchestra was injured, and not a single concert was cancelled. It was not until the orchestra was safely back in London that they had to face what was a major calamity—the destruction by enemy action in the spring of 1941 of London's principal and favourite concert-hall, known to musicians all over the world, Queen's Hall, Langham Place, W.1. The original home of the " Promenade " and Symphony Concerts, with which the name of Sir Henry Wood will always be associated, and the scene of some of the greatest triumphs of conductors of world-wide repute—Toscanini, Beecham, Nikisch, Kussevitzky, Bruno Walter, Monteux, Weingartner and many others —Queen's Hall was, in fact, the hub and focal point of the musical life of the capital. Its loss, as can readily be imagined, was therefore a most serious blow not only to the musical profession but to music-lovers everywhere.

As it happened, the London Philharmonic Orchestra was due to play there on the day following the air raid which destroyed the hall. But when the players arrived in the morning for the final rehearsal they found nothing but a burnt-out shell. To make matters worse a number of valuable instruments belonging to the musicians, which had been left at the hall over-night, had perished in the ruins, and for a time consternation reigned. But a spirit of defiance had been kindled, and in spite of everything another hall was found, and the concert took place as advertised. Instruments were borrowed from more fortunate musicians and from well-wishers, and soon the orchestra was facing life afresh. And from that day to this it has not looked back, giving concerts regularly, both in London and the provinces, and helping to keep up the high standard of orchestral playing which it shares with other leading British orchestras. It is interesting to note that the orchestra is self-supporting and managed by a committee drawn largely from the members. Before leaving the subject of the London Philharmonic, mention should be made of its founder and chief conductor, Sir Thomas Beecham. The adventures and vicissitudes outlined above were experienced by the orchestra during the early years of the war in the absence of their chief, who had had to leave England to fulfil engagements in Australia and elsewhere in the autumn of 1939. Among the many well-known conductors who conducted the London Philharmonic Orchestra during his absence may be mentioned Sir Adrian Boult, Mr. Basil Cameron, Mr. Anatole Fistoulari and Sir Malcolm Sargent, while since the liberation of France the orchestra has been privileged to play under the *bâton* of both M. Charles Munch and M. Paul Paray. Sir Thomas now conducts the newly formed orchestra of the Royal Philharmonic Society.

It is of course impossible in the space at our disposal to do full justice to all the orchestras and musical organisations which continued to function and serve the cause of music during the war; omission of any names must therefore not be taken to imply a failure to recognise the value of the good work done by all. Consequently if we cannot do more than pay an undeservedly brief tribute to the work of such distinguished bodies as the London Symphony Orchestra (one of London's oldest and best-known orchestras) and the National Symphony Orchestra, created during the war, both of which have been fully engaged in performing the best symphonic music to eager and appreciative audiences, lack of space must be our only excuse.

It would not be fair, however, to omit a special reference to the fine work of the leading orchestras in the provinces—Manchester's famous " Hallé ", the Liverpool Philharmonic, the Scottish Orchestra of Glasgow and the City of Birmingham Orchestra. The latter has been reconstituted since the war, and under its present conductor, George Weldon, has shown itself to be of excellent quality. The Liverpool Philharmonic, under its principal conductor, Sir Malcolm

Sargent, ranks high among British orchestras, and its programmes reflect the enlightened policy of the Philharmonic Society of Liverpool, which is the second oldest music society in the country, the oldest, of course, being the Royal Philharmonic Society of London—the Society which commissioned Beethoven to write his Ninth Symphony. The orchestra carried on throughout the war, giving hundreds of concerts, including some for children and for members of the Forces. It also made recordings, some of which were sponsored by the British Council—*e.g.* " Belshazzar's Feast ", by William Walton, with the Huddersfield Choir (one of Britain's best choral ensembles), conducted by the composer; the Arthur Bliss Piano Concerto with Solomon as soloist and Sir Adrian Boult conducting; Gustav Holst's " Hymn of Jesus ", and Elgar's " Dream of Gerontius ".

The record of the famous Hallé Orchestra, which has its home in Manchester, and is one of the oldest orchestras in the country, having been in existence for eighty-seven years, is also an impressive one. It now enjoys the privilege of playing regularly under the *bâton* of John Barbirolli, who has made it one of the finest orchestras in the country. The Hallé in 1944 gave 260 concerts all over the country in eleven months, and also paid a visit to France, Belgium and Holland where, under rigorous war conditions, it gave concerts to the British Liberation Army. During the blitz, when Manchester was the target for some of the fiercest attacks by the Luftwaffe, the Hallé Orchestra was deprived of its concert-hall, the Free Trade Hall, which was destroyed by bombs. The full story of the contribution made during the war by these fine orchestras cannot be related in these pages; but the inhabitants of these great industrial towns of the North are justly proud of their achievements, and have been generous in giving them unfailing support and encouragement throughout a period fraught with dangers and difficulties of every kind.

The " Proms "

A story which has to be told, however, is that of how the war affected the famous Promenade Concerts. These were the special creation of the late Sir Henry Wood, the great conductor, who died in his seventy-sixth year in the summer of 1944, only a few days before the conclusion of the fiftieth season of the " Proms ", which he had conducted almost without a break since their foundation in 1895. By his death British music sustained a serious and irreparable loss; and although the " Proms " continue under other conductors, they are still, and always will be, known as " The Henry Wood Promenade Concerts ". The debt owed by British music and musicians to this remarkable man cannot be over-estimated. In the course of his fifty years of conducting it has been estimated that 75 per cent of all the orchestral music by established native composers was given under his direction. Sir Henry, in the words of Sir Arnold Bax, which would certainly be endorsed by every other British composer of equal or lesser eminence, " has been esteemed a national institution. . . . He has purified and enriched the musical taste of at least two generations. He has improved the quality of orchestral playing out of all knowledge; and we who enjoy the high privilege of his friendship . . . must feel it an honour to have lived contemporaneously with a great man who commands not only our deepest respect and admiration but also our unqualified affection."

A tribute such as the above coming from a composer as eminent as Sir Arnold Bax serves to show with what high esteem the late Sir Henry Wood was regarded among musicians; while his faithful and enormous public worshipped him with a fervour not far removed from adoration.

A word of explanation as to the exact nature of the Promenade Concerts associated with his name should perhaps be inserted here for the benefit of any readers who may not have a clear picture in their minds of the way in which these concerts, so peculiarly a British institution, are organised. Very briefly the " Proms " (as they are invariably known and referred to in this country) are a series of orchestral concerts given nightly six times in the week over a period of eight or nine weeks during the summer months. They are called " Promenade " concerts because a large proportion of the audience listens to the music standing up, the seats on the floor of the house having been removed for this purpose. In this way the capacity of the hall is increased, which enables the price of admission to the " Promenade " to be fixed at so modest a figure as to bring these concerts within the reach of the humblest purse. But for this small expenditure (there are, of course, higher-priced seats which can be reserved) it is possible for the musical amateur to hear in one season practically the whole classical repertoire of symphonic music, with a reasonably high proportion of new contemporary works thrown in. In addition, the best soloists, singers and instrumentalists are engaged, while the programmes throughout the long season are invariably executed by our leading orchestras under the direction, since the death of Sir Henry Wood, of conductors of established repute. For many years now these concerts have been sponsored by the B.B.C., and broadcast, either wholly or in part, so that the music performed can be heard by unseen audiences vaster than those which nightly throng the hall in London where the " Proms " are given.

That, then, is the picture. Let us take our minds back now to the night of Friday, 1st September 1939. On that date the " Proms " had been running for three weeks. The orchestra engaged was the B.B.C. Symphony Orchestra. It had been arranged that, should war break out, the B.B.C. Orchestra would immediately, for security reasons, be evacuated to the country; this was merely a part of the complicated procedure to be adopted, on a signal from the Government, by the Corporation, which from that moment would be working to a pre-arranged emergency war-time schedule. Although Poland had been invaded in the early hours of the morning, the orchestra turned up as usual for rehearsal, but no one then knew whether the Promenade Concert would take place that evening. The decision was finally taken to carry on; but that was to be the last concert of that ill-fated season. The audience on leaving the hall found themselves engulfed in the first total " black-out " of the war—a black-out which was to be maintained for over five long years —and the next day the B.B.C. Symphony Orchestra had left London for its war-time base.

But the " Proms " were not dead. The following year—1940—they were held again, although the last concert of the season was brought to a sudden end by one of the Luftwaffe's fiercest raids on London. Before the 1941 season was due to begin the Queen's

Hall, the original home of the "Proms", had been destroyed, as already related, so a new home for them was found in the much larger but less suitable Albert Hall in Kensington; and there they have been ever since. Public support for these concerts showed no falling off, and audiences of 4000 to 5000 a night were by no means uncommon. Sir Henry Wood, true to his lifelong practice of encouraging contemporary music, continued to bring out new works, and in two seasons (1942–1943) no fewer than 42 works received their first performance in England at these concerts. In the summer of 1944, however, attacks by the V1 weapon—the flying bomb—began, and once more the "Proms" had to be interrupted. Those scheduled to be broadcast were performed in the studio, but the public concerts had to be discontinued. This was a great disappointment to all concerned as the season was the fiftieth to be conducted by Sir Henry, and if carried to its conclusion would have been the crowning triumph of the veteran conductor's career. The fates, however, decreed otherwise, and Sir Henry, who had for some time been in failing health, was struck down by a fatal illness and died just before the last concert of the season, which it was hoped he would be able to conduct himself, was broadcast from a studio in the country at the B.B.C. Symphony Orchestra's war-time base. Thus ended an historic chapter in the annals of British music. The "Proms", it is true, continue, but their founder and creator is no more, although his spirit still animates the work of his successors, and lives on in the affection of the public he created.

National Gallery Concerts

Looking back at the long grim years of war during which these islands were beleaguered and cut off from all contact with the continent of Europe—years of total black-out in town and country, of rationing and privations of every kind, of long hours of work and difficulties of transport and communications—it is not surprising that the people of Britain, harassed and uncertain as to their fate, should have sought solace in almost the only art that was able to survive these perilous conditions—music. For it must be remembered that for long periods theatres and most places of amusement were forced to close their doors, while picture galleries and museums had been emptied of their previous contents early in the war as a precaution against air attack. Music, however, was mobile; and musicians were not slow to see in what way they could best serve their country. At first improvisation was the order of the day, although later on, as we have seen, the musical life of the country was pretty well organised to meet the abnormal conditions imposed by the war. But a start had to be made, and it is a comforting reflection that every appeal, whether to artists to come forward and co-operate, or to the public to lend their support, invariably met with an eager and enthusiastic response.

One of the earliest musical ventures of the war, which in the long run proved as successful as any, surviving for a time the change-over from war to peace, was the organisation of the National Gallery Concerts. The idea was conceived by one of Britain's most distinguished pianists, Dame Myra Hess, who felt very strongly that one of the best ways to satisfy the public's need for mental refreshment and relaxation in the early days of the war, when all theatres, cinemas and concert-halls in London had been shut by order of the Government, would be to provide chamber-music concerts of short duration, but of high quality, daily for the benefit of war workers during their lunch hour. The question was: Where could these concerts take place? Someone suggested the National Gallery in Trafalgar Square, which was then standing empty, all the pictures having long since been evacuated to safe hide-outs in the country. On being approached, the Director, then Sir Kenneth Clark, gave his enthusiastic support to the scheme, and within a very short time permission had been obtained from the Government to use the Gallery; a committee was set up, and the first concert took place on 10th October 1939. This took the form of a piano recital given by Myra Hess, and the public's response was immediate and most encouraging. The price of admission was fixed at the nominal figure of one shilling, which was maintained throughout, and the very first concert was heard by an audience of 1000 people. During the daylight bombing of London in the autumn of 1940 it was necessary to hold the concerts in one of the Gallery's basement shelters, and the building was hit by bombs on more than one occasion. When it was necessary to evacuate, the concerts were not interrupted: they merely took place in another building. On one occasion an unexploded bomb went off in the Gallery while a concert was in progress; but no one in the audience moved, and the Stratton String Quartet continued their performance of Beethoven's F major " Rasoumovsky " quartet without missing a beat.

An enormous number of works, new and old, has been performed at these concerts, and hundreds of artists, both singers and instrumentalists, appeared on the National Gallery platform during the war years.

The programmes, designed to last about an hour, were devoted to chamber music of all kinds, instrumental and vocal; and classical music was throughout the mainstay of the repertoire. The composers who drew the largest audiences were, in fact, found to be Beethoven, Mozart and Bach. At the same time British music, old and modern, found a regular place in the programmes, and the catalogue of works performed includes the names of over a hundred British composers. In the classical repertoire a notable feature was the performance of the entire set of Mozart's 21 piano concertos, all the Beethoven quartets and violin and piano sonatas, and the complete chamber works of Brahms. Many of the concerts were broadcast to Home and Overseas listeners, and on several occasions Her Majesty the Queen was present in the audience—notably on the occasion of the 1000th concert on 23rd July 1943. In a tribute paid to Dame Myra Hess, to whose initiative these unique concerts owed their inception, the Director of the National Gallery, speaking on their third anniversary, stressed the importance of the contribution made by Dame Myra in making good music accessible to Londoners during the dreary and dangerous war years. " In all the business and distraction of a complicated enterprise," he said, "Myra Hess has not allowed the highest standards to be relaxed—never in her own playing, and never, so far as is humanly possible, in the choice of artists who play here. To maintain this sense of quality, this feeling that these are standards which must survive all disasters, is the supreme function of the arts in war-time. Those of us who are connected with the Gallery can never be sufficiently grateful for the fact that, through the art of music, it has been able to fulfil in war essentially the same purpose which it fulfilled in peace—that of maintaining through beauty our faith in the greatness of the human spirit." Without that faith it is difficult to see how the country could have survived. The part played by artists and musicians in keeping it alive cannot of course be exactly assessed, but it is certain that their efforts contributed in a very considerable measure to maintaining morale, and keeping alive among ordinary people their appreciation of those spiritual values whose very existence was endangered by the fearful impact of the war.

Sadler's Wells

As can readily be imagined, any kind of operatic enterprise had to contend with even greater handicaps and difficulties than confronted ordinary concert-giving organisations. Opera has never been a really national institution in Britain; the nearest approach to anything of the kind was achieved by the troupe known to the world as the Sadler's Wells Opera who made their home in a theatre built on the site of what was once a famous London theatre called Sadler's Wells. The late Edwin Evans, the well-known critic and writer on music, one-time President of the International Society for Contemporary Music, remarked that, " like so many English musical institutions, with the Promenade Concerts at their head, the Sadler's Wells Opera is difficult to describe because there is so little to which it can be compared. It stands several degrees nearer the Paris *Opéra-Comique* than to the Berlin *Volksoper*, but in reality it has little in common with either of these. It is a modest concern—as yet perhaps too modest to be called a national institution, though most of us look forward to its growing into one after the war. Sadler's Wells, however, has achieved something that more pretentious organisations might well envy: it has achieved singleness of purpose, complete coalescence of artistic effort."

What Sadler's Wells has to offer is, of course, very different from the grand opera which in peace-time used to be presented on a lavish scale, with international star singers and conductors, at Covent Garden. There it was the custom to give operas in their original language, with foreign singers engaged for the occasion from opera-houses all over the world; at Sadler's Wells, on the other hand, they are invariably sung in English, by British artists forming a permanent troupe. And in the years preceding the war this company was firmly established as the only permanent opera company in London, and had built up a repertory of classic and modern operas presented with great care and artistic finish and a team spirit that was wholly admirable. Their policy was progressive: for example, it was at Sadler's Wells that the British public was able to see and hear for the first time the authentic original version of "Boris Godounov" in Professor Lamm's edition published by the Soviet State Publishing Co. Another interesting venture was the presentation in the middle of the war of a new and revised staging of Smetana's "The Bartered Bride". At the second performance the entire theatre was taken by the Czechoslovak Government for the benefit of their soldiers and countrymen, whose delight at seeing an English production of their famous national opera was manifested in scenes of great enthusiasm.

Performances at Sadler's Wells, as in other London theatres, were interrupted when the air raids on the capital began in the autumn of 1940. However, a nucleus of the company was kept in being, and sent off to tour some of the smaller industrial towns not normally visited by touring companies. With an "orchestra" reduced to four, including the conductor at the piano, the entire company numbered only twenty-six; but they defied the difficulties and dangers of travelling about the country and performing in towns which frequently received the unwelcome attentions of the Luftwaffe, and continued cheerfully to present, for example, Mozart's "The Marriage of Figaro" in a *décor* consisting of two chairs and a sofa, Purcell's "Dido and Aeneas", and some of the favourite operas by Verdi and Puccini.

Before the end of the German war the company returned to London to give seasons from time to time, and as soon as hostilities ceased they settled once more in their original home at Sadler's Wells. It was here in the summer of 1945 that they produced one of the most remarkable operas ever written by a British composer—"Peter Grimes", by Benjamin Britten, which will be described later in these pages. At the moment of writing, the original Sadler's Wells company has been dissolved, but many of the artists are likely to be merged in a larger venture which will lead ultimately to the foundation for the first time in British musical history of a genuinely " National " Opera.

B.B.C.

Before we close our chapter on the activities, during the war years, of the music-makers—of all those, that is to say, who were engaged in the actual performance or organisation of music, as distinct from the composers (with whom we shall be dealing in the remaining pages of this account)—mention should be made of the important services rendered to music by the British Broadcasting Corporation (B.B.C.). The transition from peace to war necessitated a radical readjustment in every department of the B.B.C. which naturally took some time to effect. The initial difficulties, thanks to a pre-arranged plan, were, however, in due course overcome, and, after a rather groping and tentative start, by 1940 the Corporation's music programmes showed a definite improvement. It must not be forgotten that the moment hostilities were declared the broadcasting orchestras and a large proportion of the programme and administrative staffs were evacuated to the country; and at the same time many performers and artists, including orchestral players, were called up or left voluntarily to join one or other of the Forces. The B.B.C. Symphony Orchestra, for example, lost at one stroke thirty of its youngest players on the first day of the war, leaving the remaining ninety to carry on at their first war-time base which was set up at Bristol. There they stayed, with their conductor Sir Adrian Boult, until the summer of 1941. During the previous autumn and winter, Bristol became a target for the Luftwaffe, and the orchestra went through many hair-raising experiences and had many narrow escapes. One musician was killed by a bomb, and the leader of the orchestra, Paul Beard (principal violin), was once blown off his bicycle, though he escaped without serious injury. Sometimes during the bombardment the electricity would fail in the studio and the programme would have to be finished by the light of candles or oil-lamps. On one occasion, we are told, the principal violin knelt on the ground beside the microphone in a constricted underground studio to play Bach's "Air on the G String" while the bombs rained down outside. How many listeners overseas could ever have guessed under what conditions our artists were working during those dark days! And yet broadcasting went on, and though recorded programmes had sometimes to be substituted for "live" ones, they invariably went on the air as advertised and at the appointed time. In 1941 both the B.B.C. Symphony and Theatre Orchestras were moved to safer spots, and it was from Bedford, a small town in the Midlands, that the Symphony Orchestra gave all its studio broadcasts from that time until the end of the war.

Practically all the members of the orchestra joined the Home Guard, which meant that when they were not actually playing or rehearsing they were attending drills or parades, going on manœuvres or guarding the studios and broadcasting headquarters with rifles and fixed bayonets. Moreover, in addition to its regular broadcasting duties the orchestra, since 1942, undertook a series of tours in order to play to service men and women in camps and training centres all over the country, and to factory workers at their jobs. Among the places visited by the B.B.C. Symphony Orchestra were R.A.F. and Army camps in Wales and the Midlands, American camps in the West of England, the important naval centres of Portsmouth and Southampton, and the famous military establishment, Aldershot. In addition to the more popular classical masterpieces, for which there was everywhere a great demand, the programmes included works by such composers as Sibelius, Debussy, Vaughan Williams, Delius, Elgar and Holst, which were everywhere listened to with eagerness and real appreciation. Many stories are told of the interest aroused among the men and their reactions to hearing music of this quality played by a first-rate symphony orchestra. For example, there was that R.A.F. sergeant in Wales who, after hearing a rehearsal of a Symphony by Sibelius, said he had never had such a thrill in his life—"I shall be at every concert," he exclaimed; "I only wish they went on for weeks." Many of the men who listened to these concerts in the camps had come to England to fight from overseas, like that dark-skinned soldier from Jamaica who wanted Sir Adrian Boult's photograph, and in asking for it made the following little speech: " I cannot tell you the pleasure I have had. I come from Jamaica where I used to make music myself. I get little opportunity now in the Army either to make or listen to music. So it has been a privilege today for me—that music and that playing. Thank you, sir, thank you very much." If further proof be needed that good music is appreciated by a far wider public than that which regularly attends concerts, it is on record that in one camp the famous pianist Solomon, in the course of a recital he was giving to the troops, asked his audience what he should play. One half demanded the " Appassionata " sonata of Beethoven, the other half the " Waldstein ". . . . But of course the main work of the B.B.C. Symphony Orchestra and the other broadcasting orchestras, Theatre, Variety, Revue, as well as of the B.B.C. Singers (chorus-master, Leslie Woodgate) and of the many solo artists and chamber-music ensembles who appeared regularly before the microphone, was carried on from the studio. From here they broadcast not only to Home listeners, but also to Europe and to America, North and South, India, and all the countries of the British Commonwealth. There was, in fact, scarcely a spot on the globe that did not hear, even during the darkest days of the war, the musical voice of Britain. And in the programmes broadcast, some place was always found for contemporary British music, as the following list of only a few of the many British works, broadcast or performed for the first time by the B.B.C., will show:

William Walton
- Prelude and " Spitfire " Fugue
- Violin Concerto
- Incidental Music to " Macbeth "
- Overture " Scapino ".
- Christopher Columbus

John Ireland
- Epic March
- Three Pastels for Piano
- " These Things Shall Be "

E. J. Moeran
- Violin Concerto
- Rhapsody for Piano and Orchestra

Vaughan Williams
- Symphony No. 5 in D
- Incidental Music to Bunyan's " Pilgrim's Progress "
- Victory Anthem

Benjamin Britten
- 7 Sonnets of Michelangelo
- Hymn to St. Cecilia
- Sinfonia da Requiem
- A Ceremony of Carols
- " Peter Grimes "

Edmund Rubbra
- Symphony No. 4
- Introduction and Dance

Alan Rawsthorne
- Piano Concerto
- Incidental Music to Red Army programme

Arnold Bax
- Film Music: " Malta, G.C."
- Symphony No. 7 (1st Concert performance in London)
- Violin Concerto
- Legend

Arthur Bliss
- String Quartet

Michael Tippett
- Second String Quartet
- Cantata: " Boyhood's End "
- Oratorio: " A Child of Our Time "

Constant Lambert
- Aubade Héroïque

Lennox Berkeley
- Symphony
- Four Concert Studies

This list does not pretend to include more than a few works by the more important British composers. Among outstanding foreign works broadcast by the B.B.C. may be mentioned: "Symphony in C" and "Apollo Musagetes", Stravinsky; "Festival Mass", Janaček; Violin Concerto, Bartók; "Leningrad" and Eighth Symphonies, Shostakovich; Symphony in E flat, Hindemith; Symphony No. 3, Roy Harris; and works by Honegger, Roussel, Prokofiev, etc. etc.

In 1940 the B.B.C. Symphony Orchestra was conducted by Albert Wolff, who came over from Paris just before the Fall of France; by Gregor Fitelberg from Poland; and by the Belgian conductor Désiré Defauw; and in the winter of 1943 it had the privilege of playing at a public concert under the eminent Portuguese conductor from Lisbon, Pedro de Freitas Branco. This concert was relayed by Emisora Nacional and aroused the greatest interest in both British and Portuguese musical circles. Then in the autumn of 1944, after the liberation of France, musical relations between Britain and France were happily restored, after an interruption of five years, by the visit to this country of such distinguished musicians as Charles Munch and Paul Paray, both of whom conducted the B.B.C. Symphony Orchestra in concerts that were broadcast; while the B.B.C.'s chief conductor, Sir Adrian Boult, went to Paris the following spring to conduct the Orchestre de la Société des Concerts du Conservatoire and the Orchestre National de la Radiodiffusion Française. Francis Poulenc and Pierre Bernac also revisited England, and Poulenc's cantata "Figure Humaine" received its first world performance when it was broadcast, in an English translation, by the B.B.C. Singers, conductor Leslie Woodgate, in March 1945. Among the soloists who came over from Paris to broadcast for the B.B.C. were Yvonne Lefébure and Nicole Henriot, pianists, and Ginette Neveu, violinist, all of whom had a warm welcome. With the restoration of peace it is to be hoped that a free interchange of artists of all nations will speedily become a reality again, and that British music will find its way to other lands while we in Britain may learn more of what our neighbours have been doing since communications were interrupted by the war.

British Council

It is in this field that the British Council has a part to play, and our readers may be interested to hear what the Council's Music Department has accomplished since its inception some ten years ago. One of its principal activities has been the establishment of Music Libraries in various countries abroad where British works are constantly available, either in the form of gramophone records or in print. The largest and best equipped of these libraries, of which there are no less than fifty-seven now functioning in various parts of the world, are at present in Stockholm, Cairo and Buenos Aires. In the Stockholm library alone some seventy-five British composers, both living and dead, are represented. In Portugal, Scandinavia and Latin America especially the keenest interest is taken in British music, while there is scarcely a country, from China to Peru, where the Council has not set up some organisation to render our music accessible, in some form or other, to local amateurs and professional bodies wishing to hear or perform it. Since the formation of the Council's Music Department, for example, no fewer than 500 major works by British composers have been hired and sent abroad. At the same time the Council has made itself responsible for a number of special recordings of outstanding works by British composers which have since been circulated throughout the world.

The list of these includes 98 copies of William Walton's "Belshazzar's Feast", 88 of the Bliss Piano Concerto, 85 of Moeran's Symphony in G minor, 82 of Bax's Third Symphony, 77 of the Fifth Symphony of Vaughan Williams, and 75 of Holst's "The Hymn of Jesus". This collection has recently been increased by the addition of the following recordings, specially sponsored by the Council: Elgar's "The Dream of Gerontius"; "The Planets" by Gustav Holst; Purcell's "Dido and Aeneas"; Rawsthorne's "Street Corner"; Bliss's "Phoenix" March.

Many of the records thus disseminated abroad are used by foreign broadcasting stations, and as a result British music is now reaching the ears of hundreds of thousands of people all over the world who might otherwise never have had an opportunity of hearing it. Among radio stations which have been supplied with records, in addition to those in outlying parts of the Empire such as the A.B.C.

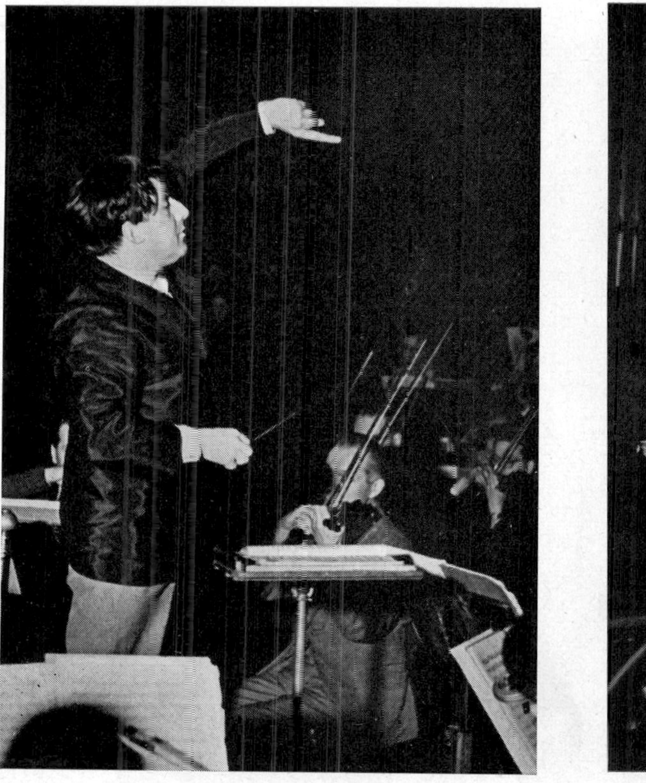

John Barbirolli, the conductor of the Hallé Orchestra

Sir Adrian Boult, with Paul Beard, leader of the B.B.C. Symphony Orchestra, and Marie Wilson, former first violinist

Dame Myra Hess playing at a war-time National Gallery Concert

The late Edwin Evans

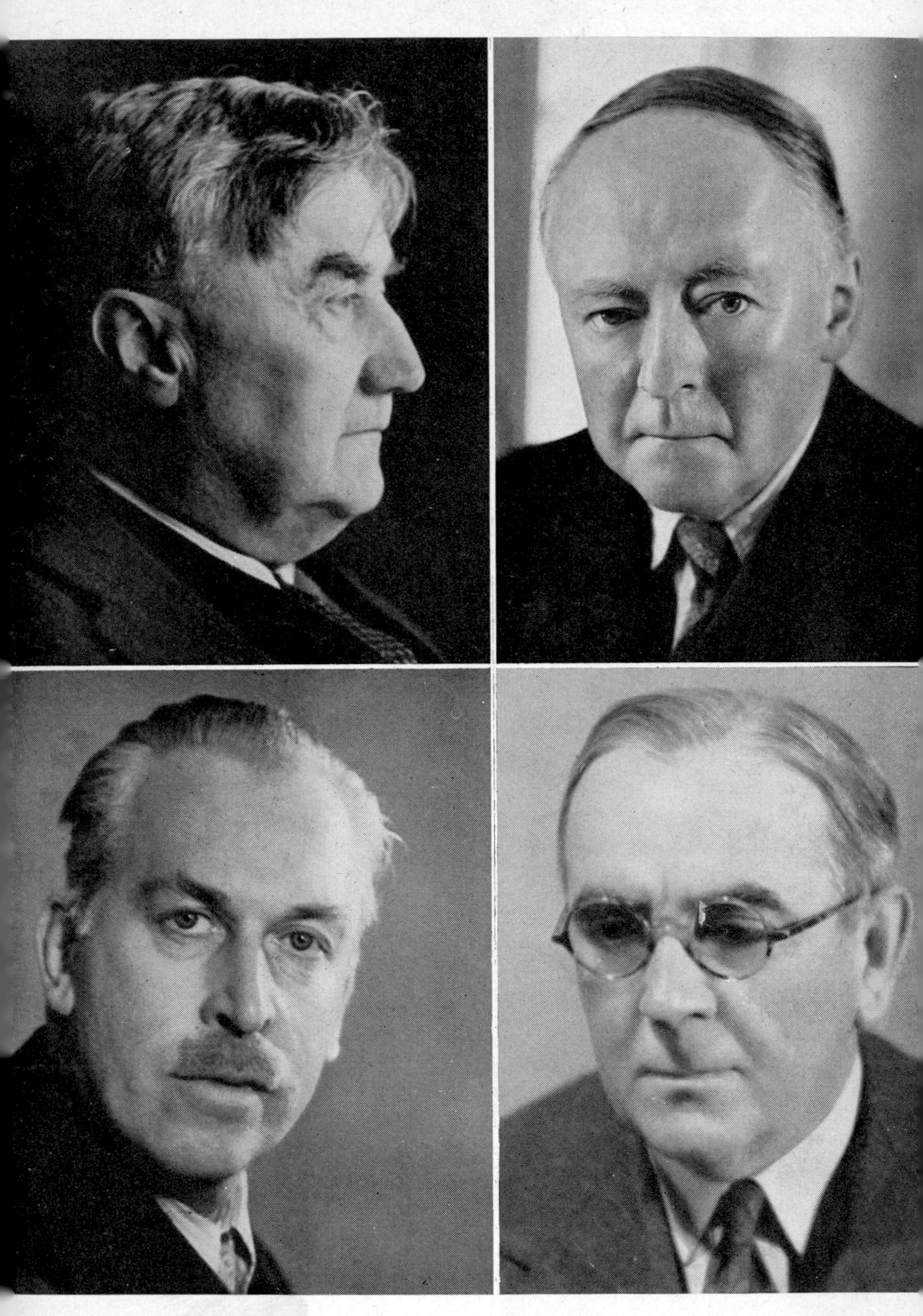

Above: Ralph Vaughan Williams
Below: Arthur Bliss

Above: Sir Arnold Bax, Master of the King's M
Below: John Ireland

of Australia and stations in Africa and B.W.I., may be mentioned Radio Provincia, of Buenos Aires; Radio Levant, Syria; the Broadcasting station of Jerusalem, and the Icelandic State Broadcasting Station.

Furthermore, the Council has been instrumental in securing live performances of important British works in many places abroad, so that we read of Purcell's " Golden Sonata " being performed in Argentina and in Mauritius ; of Bliss's " Things to Come " played at three concerts in Bari; and of performances of Britten, Vaughan Williams and Walton in Paris, Palestine, Sweden, Portugal, Trinidad, Chile and Uruguay. And the list could be almost indefinitely extended.

Some of the keenest admirers of British music are to be found in the South American Republics, and three thousand works have been sent to Argentina alone. Russia, too, is taking an increasing interest in our music, there being a great demand for our folk-songs, many of which have been recently arranged by Soviet composers and sung by the Red Army Choir and other choral societies. It is gratifying, too, to be able to record that the 250th anniversary of the death of Purcell was celebrated in March 1946 in Moscow by a performance of " Dido and Aeneas " which took place at the Home of Scientists under the direction of Professor Sadovnikov; while lectures on contemporary British music have been given by Igor Boelza and others. We learn, too, that the great Russian violinist Oistrach is adding to his repertoire Elgar's Violin Concerto.

Before concluding this necessarily brief survey of the British Council's work on behalf of British music and musicians, which includes, of course, giving facilities to British artists enabling them to give concerts in important centres all over the world, mention should be made of one more of the Council's undertakings which was found during the war to be of the greatest value to foreigners desiring to become better acquainted with our music. A Library of Gramophone Records was formed in this country for the benefit of members of foreign missions and service men and women stationed over here upon which they could draw when arranging programmes in camps, clubs, etc., for their own nationals. The

Council made a point of including at least one British work in every parcel sent out, and the scheme proved very popular—how popular may be judged from the fact that from 25 to 30 parcels of records were dispatched from this library every day.

It may be seen from the above bird's-eye view of what the British Council has done and is doing for British music that the good seed already sown has by no means fallen on stony ground.

II. COMPOSERS

As can be readily imagined, the war years were not particularly propitious to composers of serious music in Britain. The general disorganisation of life, the material discomfort and dangers during the periods of sustained air attack, and the mental and physical strain from which anyone living under these conditions, and especially artists, were bound to suffer were not, on the whole, conducive to creative work of any kind. Nevertheless many of our leading composers managed to do good work, and in some cases had the satisfaction of seeing it performed during the war.[1] Let us consider, first of all, four of Britain's best-known composers who are all today over the age of fifty and see what they managed to produce since 1939.

The doyen of British composers, Ralph Vaughan Williams (b. 1872), although engaged on war work of various kinds in the country locality where he lives, nevertheless found time to write during the war years several major works. First amongst these must be placed his Fifth Symphony, a truly noble work epitomising in a mood of, for the most part, sustained serenity the accumulated experiences of a long life of single-hearted devotion to the art of music. In a sense the symphony could be described as a synthesis, a summing-up of the composer's musical outlook and aspirations expressed in his own unmistakable idiom, ripened now to a splendid maturity. The Fifth Symphony was broadcast on its first performance at a Promenade Concert in London in the summer of 1943, the composer conducting. Other compositions of note by Vaughan Williams during the period under review include an Oboe Concerto, a

[1] For works which have been recorded, see Appendix, p. 140.

String Quartet, and a work for chorus, speaker and orchestra entitled " Thanksgiving for Victory ", which was first performed and broadcast on 8th May 1945—the " Victory in Europe " Day which marked the end of the German war.

Vaughan Williams, like many of our younger composers, does not scorn to write music for the cinema; and among films which have benefited from his distinguished collaboration are " 49th Parallel ", " Coastal Command " and " The Story of a Flemish Farm ". A suite arranged from the latter was performed under the composer's direction at a Promenade Concert in the summer of 1945.

In 1942 Dr. Vaughan Williams celebrated his seventieth birthday, and to mark the occasion a number of British composers wrote works in the form of a tribute to one of the greatest and universally respected figures in contemporary music, and six special concerts were broadcast in his honour.

Sir Arnold Bax (b. 1883) has for long been one of the foremost figures in British music. He is also one of the most prolific, counting among his musical " baggage " no less than seven symphonies, numerous tone-poems, some important choral works, several concertos, and a substantial body of chamber works, songs and piano music. He was knighted in 1937, and in 1942 was made Master of the King's Musick, an ancient Court appointment which carries with it the duty of supervising the music used at ceremonial State occasions. The post was created in the seventeenth century, in the reign of Charles II, and among the distinguished musicians who have borne the title since its foundation we find the names of John Eccles (1650–1735), William Boyce (1710–1799), Sir Edward Elgar (1857–1934) and Walford Davies (1869–1941).

Bax's output since 1939 has not been large, but in 1941 he was commissioned to write the music for a film picturing the defence of Malta, which has been broadcast as a symphonic item. Mention should be made, too, of two short orchestral works, recently completed, entitled " Legend " and " Work in Progress ", and a sonata for 'cello and piano (" Legend ")—all of which have been performed during the war. Bax has also written an " Ode to Russia " for chorus and orchestra, and a set of " Five Fantasies on Polish Christmas Carols " for treble voice and string orchestra. His very latest published compositions are two works for choir and organ—" Te Deum " and " Nunc Dimittis ".

On the eve of his sixtieth birthday Sir Arnold's Seventh Symphony was broadcast, and on St. Cecilia's Day, 22nd November 1943, his Violin Concerto received its first performance. The soloist was the late Eda Kersey, one of Britain's leading violinists, whose death during the war was a great loss to British music, and the work was broadcast by the B.B.C.

Since 1940 Sir Arnold Bax has been living in a quiet village in the South of England.

John Ireland (b. 1879) was another of the pioneers of the British musical revival which set in about the beginning of the twentieth century, and his compositions have greatly enriched the modern repertoire. His piano and chamber music rank high in the estimation of the best critics; among his major works may be cited the Concerto for Piano and Orchestra, and the big choral work " These Things Shall Be ". When war broke out, Ireland was living in the Channel Islands, on the island of Guernsey, but managed to escape in June 1940 shortly before the German occupation. He brought with him the unfinished sketch of his piano work entitled " Sarnia: an Island Sequence " (Sarnia being the old Roman name for Guernsey), which he completed the following year. This has been performed and broadcast a number of times, as has also the " Epic March " for full orchestra which was commissioned by the B.B.C. Other works dating from this period include a setting of the Morning and Evening Canticles of the Anglican Church, and a set of pieces for the piano entitled " Three Pastels ". Later works include a Fantasy-Sonata for clarinet and piano, and a " Maritime Overture " for Military Band. Ireland also wrote some smaller vocal pieces, including one for treble voices and piano entitled " Ex ore Innocentium ". The composer tells us that none of the above works can be said to be in any way connected with the war, with the possible exception of the " Epic March ", which might be taken to suggest some opposition to Nazism and Fascism.

One of the best-known names among contemporary British composers is that of Arthur Bliss (b. 1891). His early works, which began to appear about 1920, attracted considerable attention,

They were provocative, original and full of a most refreshing vitality and unconventionality. Since then his style has greatly matured, although his music is still characterised by these same qualities. His latest works exhibit a remarkable technical proficiency, amounting to a complete command of whatever medium he adopts, and a dynamic rhythmic vitality, combined with a directness of approach, free from any suspicion of insincerity or misplaced emotionalism, from which emerges the impression of an arresting, fully equipped musical personality who has something to say and knows exactly how to say it. When the war broke out Bliss was in America, having been appointed Professor of Music at the University of California. In 1941, however, in response to an invitation from the B.B.C., he returned to England to become, firstly, Assistant Director of Overseas Music, and then Director of Music in the Corporation—a post which he resigned in 1944.

His most important compositions during this period have been the ballets " Miracle in the Gorbals " and " Adam Zero ", both produced by the Sadler's Wells Ballet Company, and the music for two films—" Men of Two Worlds " and " La France Combattante ". His march " The Phoenix ", in honour of France, has been performed in Paris under Charles Munch, since the liberation, and recently recorded.

Finally, mention should be made of his " Seven American Poems " for voice and piano, and a fine String Quartet composed before he left California at the invitation of Mrs. Elizabeth Sprague Coolidge, and first performed at the University of California in 1941 by the Pro Arte Quartet. In England this has been played and recorded by the Griller Quartet.

The music of William Walton (b. 1902) is probably better known abroad than that of almost any other living British composer. His Symphony, his Concertos for Violin and for Viola, his suite " Façade ", the overtures " Portsmouth Point " and " Scapino " and the big choral work " Belshazzar's Feast " are among his best-known works and have made him an outstanding figure in contemporary British music.

The Violin Concerto, completed just before the war, had its first performance in Cleveland, U.S.A., in December 1939, with

Heifetz as soloist; and " Scapino ", written for the Chicago Symphony Orchestra's fiftieth anniversary, was completed in 1940 and performed there the following year. Other works of this period were " Music for Children ", the ballet " The Wise Virgins " (orchestration of music by Bach), and music for the film " Major Barbara " (Bernard Shaw).

The greater part of Walton's output during the war was, at the behest of the Ministry of Labour and National Service, confined to films, to be produced under the auspices of either the War Office or the Ministry of Information. Chief among these must be counted " Next of Kin ", " The First of the Few " (dealing with the life of the inventor of the Spitfire) and, last but not least, Shakespeare's " Henry V ", the film which provided the major cinematographic sensation of the year 1944. In 1943, however, Walton was able to find time, apart from his official duties, to write the music for a ballet, " The Quest ", and the incidental music for John Gielgud's production of " Macbeth ".

Another composer of note who has had to combine music with military service is Edmund Rubbra (b. 1901), who, as a sergeant in the British Army of Liberation in Germany, was until recently in charge of the Army Music Group. The object of the Music Group, which includes several performers of note, is to give the troops an opportunity of hearing the very best chamber music. These musicians in battle-dress have undertaken tours of camps and training centres in England and Scotland, and are now doing the same in Germany, playing for the Army of Occupation.

Rubbra has written four notable Symphonies, the last of which was completed during the war and first performed at a Promenade Concert in London in 1942. His more recent works include a " Soliloquy " (for solo 'cello, string orchestra, 2 horns and tympani) and a " Mass " for double choir which was commissioned for Canterbury Cathedral. Rubbra's music is original without being eccentric in any way: in the words of a contemporary critic, " he reaches out to new fields of expression while keeping one foot in the ancient ways ". One of the best and most attractive of his chamber works is the Second Violin and Piano Sonata; while his " Sinfonia Concertante ", for piano and orchestra, revised and performed since the war, with the composer playing the solo part, must be counted as one of his major works.

Coming now to the younger generation, we find a number of most talented composers of whom perhaps the most prominent at the present time is Benjamin Britten (b. 1913). Britten's rise to fame has been rapid, following a brilliantly precocious youthful period during which he produced works exhibiting an astonishing technical facility which at one time threatened to outstrip the quality of his musical thought. In his latest works, however, that danger has been dispelled and his art is developing in a way that seems to justify the highest hopes. One of his earliest works to attract the attention of musicians outside his native country was the Quartet for Oboe and Strings performed in 1934 at the Florence Festival of the I.S.C.M. Britten was then aged twenty-one. Then came the "Variations on a Theme of Frank Bridge" which gained for him in 1938 an international reputation. (Frank Bridge, who died in 1940, was a British composer of note who gave Britten his first serious musical instruction and remained his adviser and friend until his death; later Britten studied composition at the Royal College of Music in London under John Ireland.) Among his best-known later works are the "Sinfonia da Requiem" (first performed in New York under Barbirolli in 1941), the First String Quartet, the "Sonnets of Michelangelo" for tenor and piano; the song-cycle "Les Illuminations" (a setting of words by Rimbaud) and the "Serenade" for tenor, horn and strings. The first four of these works were composed or completed in America, where Britten remained from 1939 to 1942; the "Serenade", one of his finest achievements to date, was written after his return to England. His war-time and post-war output also includes three choral works: "Hymn to St. Cecilia" for mixed voices *a cappella*, to words written by the poet W. H. Auden; "A Ceremony of Carols", for treble voices and harp or piano; a festival cantata, "Rejoice in the Lamb", for mixed voices and organ, and the Second String Quartet.

All the above-mentioned works are published and have been performed in the U.S.A., in England and on the continent of Europe.

But perhaps the most outstanding of all his works to date is the opera "Peter Grimes", which was first produced in London by the Sadler's Wells Opera Company in June 1945. Composed to a libretto by Montagu Slater after the poem by the eighteenth-century "realist" English poet George Crabbe, the opera provides a musical background to a story of a somewhat uncompromising realism in which the protagonist is a sadist fisherman, Peter Grimes, whose brutalities towards the workhouse boys who become his apprentices arouse the anger and indignation of his fellow villagers, who finally drive Grimes to commit suicide. This he does by putting out to sea in his boat and scuttling it. The action takes place in a seaside village on the East Coast of England in and around the market square and tavern; and into the tragic events of the story are woven the changing moods of the sea and the violent emotional reactions of the villagers towards the man whom they feel to be a monster, but into whose spiritual loneliness (the cause of his excesses) they are unable to penetrate. For Grimes is a dual personality—and to suggest this has been one of the composer's main objectives. The opera abounds in moments of extraordinary power and poignancy, and the choral writing, expressing the collective soul of the little township, is no less remarkable than the solo declamatory parts assigned to the chief actors, and the rich and subtle orchestral score which contributes so largely to the opera's overwhelming effect upon the spectator. The orchestral Interludes from the opera have been arranged for concert performance as a Suite, and can be performed separately. "Peter Grimes" is probably Britten's finest achievement to date, and has aroused great interest among both musicians and the general public, who evidently found the work to its liking. The first performance on the Continent of this striking new British opera took place at Stockholm in March 1946, and this was followed, in the same year, by performances at Basle, Zürich, Antwerp and Boston, U.S.A.[1]

It should be added that Britten is a brilliant pianist and, in addition to composing, devotes much of his time to performing, appearing frequently as either solo pianist, accompanist or conductor.

[1] A more recent "chamber opera", with an orchestra of only eleven instruments and percussion, on the story of "The Rape of Lucretia", had its first performance in England in 1946, and a comic opera, "Albert Herring", in 1947.

cene from Benjamin Britten's opera "Peter Grimes": Peter Pears as Peter Grimes, Joan Cross as Ellen Orford, Leonard Thompson as the Apprentice Boy

(Photo: *Peggy Delius*)

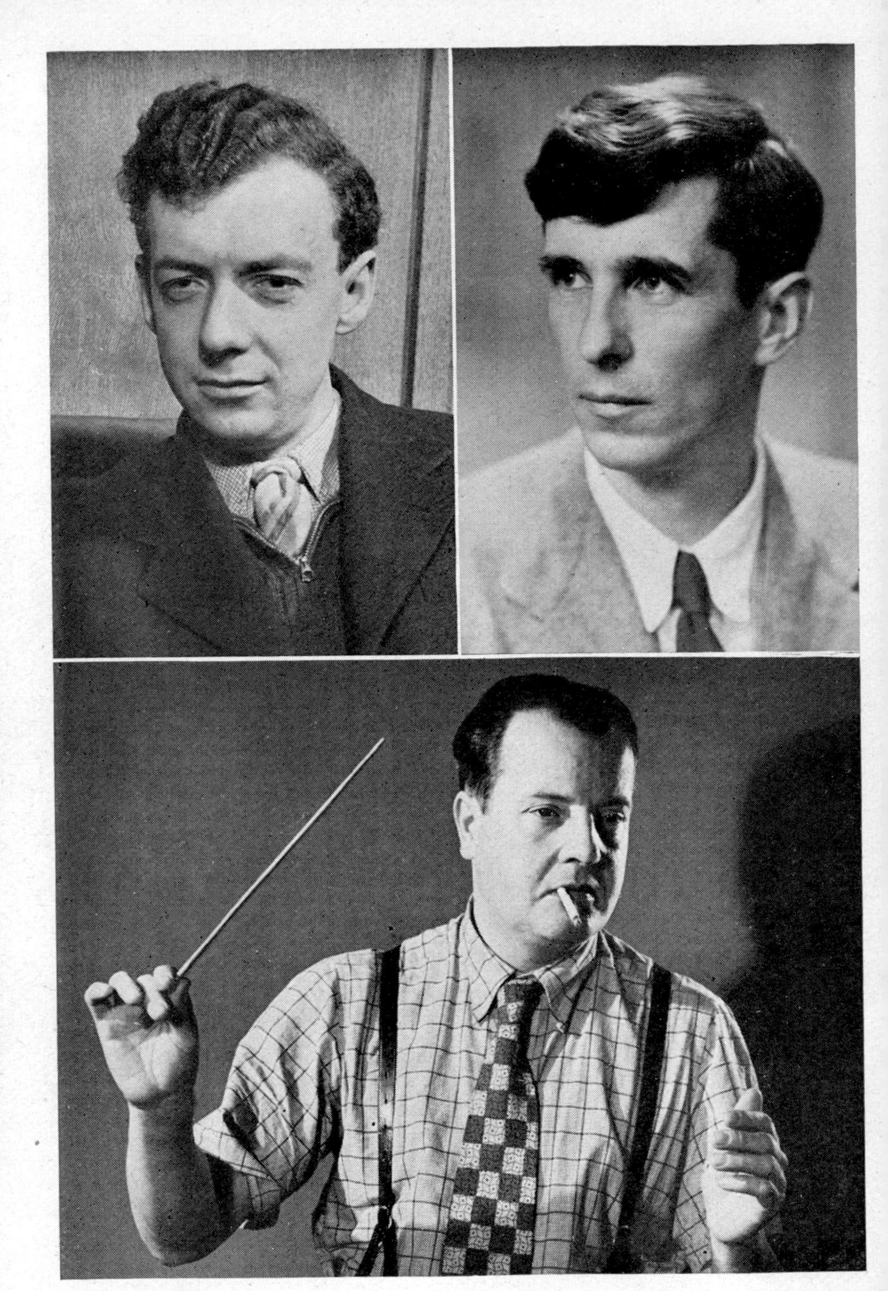

Benjamin Britten Constant Lambert Michael Tippett

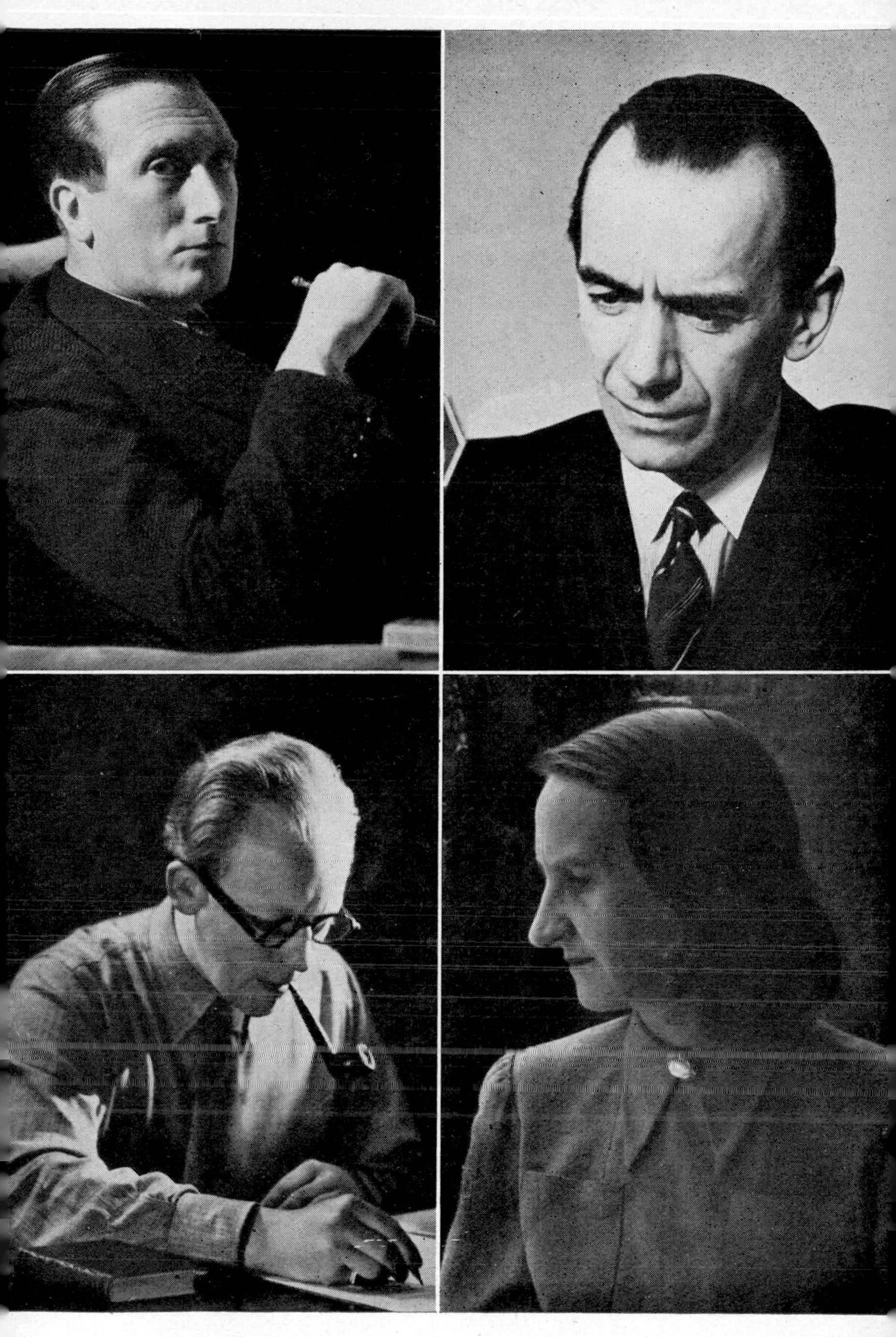

Above: William Walton
Below: Alan Rawsthorne

Above: Sir Malcolm Sargent
Below: Elizabeth Lutyens
(Photo: *Vogu*

Yehudi Menuhin

Rehearsal of the Boyd Neel String Orchestra

EDMUND RUBBRA (Photo: *Peggy Delius*)

The Huddersfield Choral Society

A famous English musical family—Sidonie and Marie Goossens, harpists of the B.B.C. and London Symphony Orchestras, Eugene, composer-conductor, and Leon, solo oboist

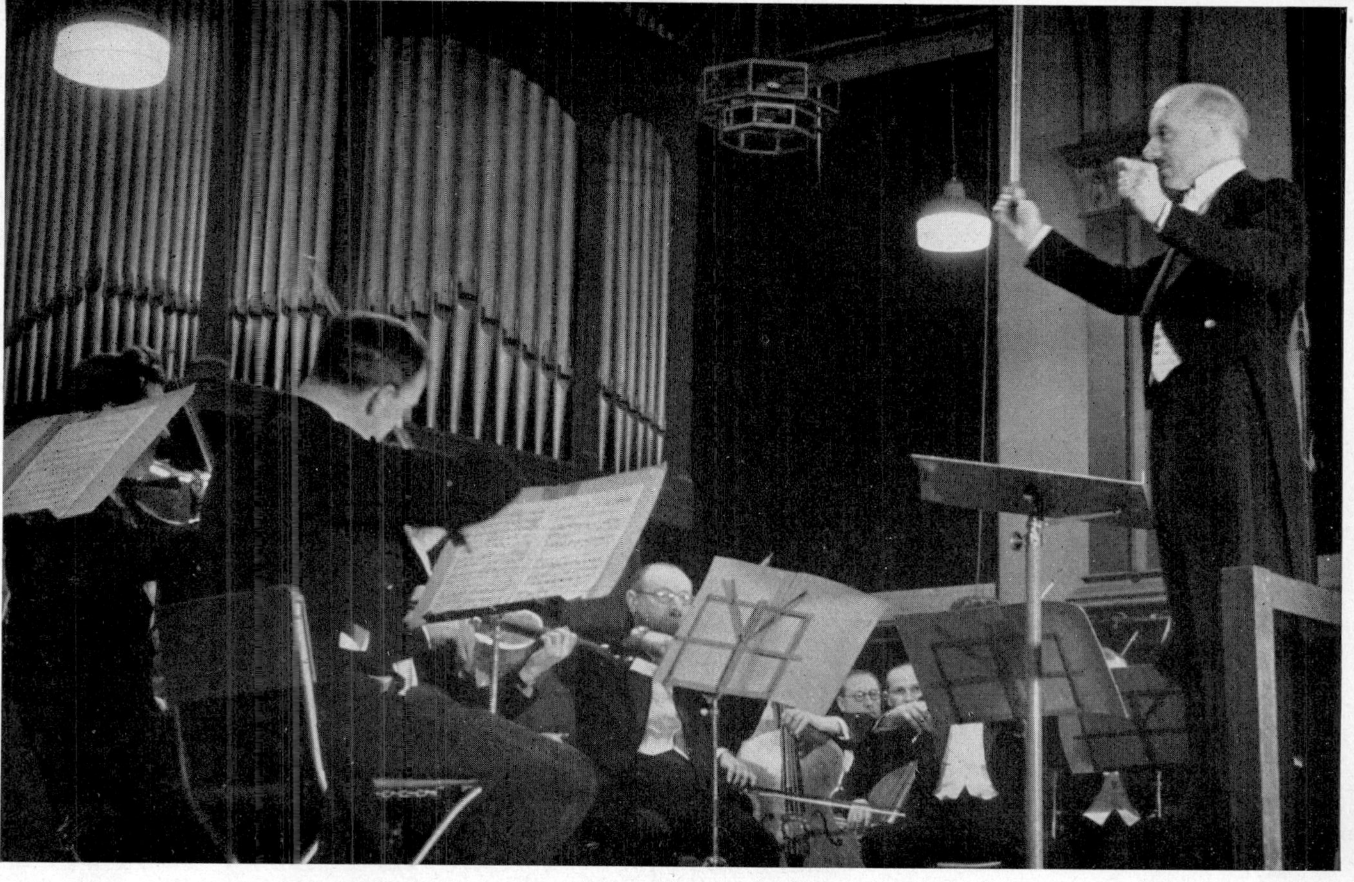

Sir Adrian Boult conducting the B.B.C. Symphony Orchestra

The new home of the "Proms": the Royal Albert Hall

He very often partners the tenor Peter Pears, who, besides singing Britten's songs, played the part of Peter Grimes in the opera.

It was for Britten and Pears that Michael Tippett (b. 1905), another composer who is now making a name for himself, wrote in 1943 his cantata for tenor and piano, "Boyhood's End". The cantata was broadcast in 1945, and the composer considers it to be one of his most representative works. Tippett is now Director of Music at Morley College, in South London, an institution which caters for students drawn from the working and professional classes—where music is a prominent feature of the curriculum. The College building was badly damaged by a land-mine in 1940, but work goes on, and the concerts given there are attended by an enthusiastic group of young people, professionals and amateurs. When the war broke out Tippett was working on his "Fantasia for Piano and Orchestra on a Theme of Handel", and had written the words of his oratorio "A Child of Our Time", which is one of his major works. This was completed in the spring of 1941, and produced three years later in London. The "hero" of this oratorio, which presents many unfamiliar features—for example, some of the choruses take the form of "Negro Spirituals"—was the Polish Jew, Grynspan, who assassinated an official at the German Embassy in Paris in 1938. The work had considerable success, and has since been performed outside London and broadcast by the B.B.C. It has also been broadcast from Brussels. During the war it was performed in London at a concert organised by the Polish Government in aid of their orphans. Other important works of Tippett are his Second String Quartet (produced in 1943) and the Concerto for Double String Orchestra. His most recent works are his Symphony No. 2, which had its *première* at a concert given by the Liverpool Philharmonic Society in November 1945, and the Third String Quartet.

Tippett cultivates a certain austerity of style, and his music tends in the main to be contrapuntal and polyphonic, though by no means devoid of emotional intensity. In the words of a contemporary critic, "he is the only considerable composer I call to mind who has somehow managed to by-pass the nineteenth century—at all events as exhibited in its most characteristic features. His contemporaneity, therefore, rests partly on the revival of musical textures and idioms that recall those of the second half of the sixteenth century, and partly on a certain 'prophetic' quality which is as difficult to pin down as Britten's medievalism, but which disengages itself powerfully in the experience of listening to his music. Michael Tippett, even more essentially perhaps than Britten, belongs to the future of music."

Another young composer who is attracting a good deal of attention today is Alan Rawsthorne (b. 1905). His very great gifts did not reveal themselves to the outside world until he was over thirty (he did not begin to study music seriously until he was twenty), when a work of his was performed at the London Festival of the International Society for Contemporary Music. This was the "Theme and Variations" for two violins; at the next Festival, held in Warsaw just before war broke out, there was a first performance of his "Symphonic Studies" for orchestra, a strikingly original and characteristic work, revealing the composer's grasp of form and the conciseness of his musical thinking. Among his writings for the piano the "Bagatelles" are probably the best known, but his finest achievement to date is the Concerto for Piano and Orchestra—a work which has already been heard in Paris and is establishing itself in the repertoire of leading pianists of the day. During the war Rawsthorne was in uniform and his musical activities were practically confined to writing music for Army Films—a task which he accomplished with the greatest proficiency and brilliance. He managed to find time, however, outside his military duties, to write an orchestral piece, "Cortèges", which had its *première* at a Promenade Concert in London in 1945, and to re-score the Piano Concerto—which he did very largely while working in the Quarter-Master's office! He also has in preparation a Concerto for Violin, the original MS. of which was destroyed when his flat was hit by a bomb during the London "blitz", and has recently completed an overture for E.N.S.A. entitled "Street Corner". In the meantime musicians everywhere will be awaiting with eagerness the next work from his pen, for Rawsthorne is a composer who will undoubtedly make his mark.

The same remark applies, one feels, to Lennox Berkeley (b. 1903), who received the major part of his musical training in Paris from the celebrated French composer, conductor and teacher, Mlle Nadia Boulanger. Berkeley's music has an unmistakable Gallic flavour, as might be expected in view of his training and residence in Paris for a period of over six years; but in his most recent works his personality is establishing itself more firmly while his style matures. Berkeley has written a good deal of music since 1939, in spite of having been on the staff of the B.B.C. since 1942. His orchestral works include a Symphony, which has been performed at a " Prom " in London, with the composer conducting; a " Divertimento " (commissioned by the B.B.C.); and music for two films: " Hotel Reserve " and " Out of Chaos ". He has also been particularly active in the field of chamber music, having written a String Trio, Second String Quartet, a Sonatina for Violin and Piano, a Sonata for Viola and Piano, and a Sonata for Piano Solo. Previous to the war he had written an oratorio, " Jonah " (broadcast in 1936), and music for a ballet, " The Judgment of Paris ", produced at Sadler's Wells in 1938. He has also had works performed at Festivals of the I.S.C.M. in Barcelona and London.

The name of Constant Lambert (b. 1905) is familiar to musicians both in and outside Britain on account of his great versatility as composer, conductor and author of one of the best books on modern music, *Music Ho!* Lambert's name first came before the international public in 1926 when his ballet " Romeo and Juliet ", which had been commissioned by Diaghileff, was performed by the Russian Ballet at Monte Carlo. Three years later came " The Rio Grande " for solo piano, chorus and orchestra on a poem by Sacheverell Sitwell which still remains one of his most characteristic works. His masterpiece, however, is probably the Masque for orchestra, chorus and baritone solo, with words by the Elizabethan poet Thomas Nashe, entitled " Summer's Last Will and Testament ". This is a thoroughly mature, finely balanced and imaginatively conceived work, which shows the composer at the height of his powers. For some years now Lambert has devoted a large part of his time to conducting and until recently was musical director and chief conductor of the Sadler's Wells Ballet, which is a great feature of London life. He has himself written two ballets — " Horoscope " and

" Pomona ", but since 1939 he has done more conducting than composing. In 1940 he was in Holland touring with the Sadler's Wells Ballet Company when the German invasion of the Netherlands was launched, but managed to escape with all the other artists in the nick of time. As it was they had to leave behind much of their valuable scenery and stage property. This experience inspired Lambert to write his " Aubade Héroïque " for orchestra, the idea of which came to him while he was standing on the quay at Rotterdam waiting for the boat to take him back to England, and watching the sun rise over the Dutch landscape. Another of Lambert's wartime compositions takes the form of an orchestral suite from the music he wrote for a film called " Merchant Seamen ".

Constant Lambert has often appeared as a conductor on the Continent—for example, he conducted William Walton's " Belshazzar's Feast " at the I.S.C.M. Festival in Amsterdam in 1933, and in 1937 he went with the Sadler's Wells Ballet to Paris to conduct the special performances they gave at the Exhibition. He was in Paris again in the spring of 1945 when the ballet appeared at the Théâtre des Champs-Élysées. Later in the year he made his first appearance as Associate Conductor of the London Promenade Concerts, sharing duties with Sir Adrian Boult and Mr. Basil Cameron.

E. J. Moeran (b. 1894) is a composer who has increased his output considerably since 1939, having produced a Violin Concerto (1942), a Rhapsody for Piano and Orchestra (1943), an " Overture to a Masque " (1944), a " Sinfonietta " (1944) and a Concerto for Violoncello and Orchestra (1945). His music is refreshingly free from pretension, and is the reflection of a musical personality drawing its inspiration from nature and sensitive to the appeal of the folk element in the music of his native land.

Our gallery of musicians would not be complete without some mention of the composer Patrick Hadley (b. 1899), who is a Doctor of Music at Cambridge University, where he is now Lecturer in Music and Fellow of Gonville and Caius College. Most of Hadley's compositions are choral, one of his most important being a Symphony of three orchestral movements with a vocal finale entitled " The Trees so High ". This is scored for large orchestra with baritone solo and mixed chorus. Since the war he has been, as he expresses it, "engrossed in helping to keep the musical flag flying in Cambridge", where besides lecturing he took over the duties of conductor of the Cambridge University Musical Society. Performances under his *bâton* included Beethoven's "Mass in D", the Mozart "Requiem", the Brahms Violin Concerto, "Appalachia" and "Song of the High Hills" by Delius, and the first performance of his own latest important work, "Travellers". This was written during the war, and is dedicated to the men who left Cambridge to serve their country. This has been broadcast, and was performed at a Promenade Concert in London in the summer of 1945. Another large-scale work from his pen, for chorus, orchestra and eight soloists, is now complete. This is called "The Hills". Hadley is a sensitive musician with a great feeling for the English language and the English landscape, and occasionally makes effective use of folk idiom.

The musical Renaissance in Britain, so noticeable since the turn of the century, has been marked by the advent of several women composers whose works command attention. A pioneer in this field was the late Dame Ethel Smyth (1858-1944), who wrote among other things several operas, the best known of which are "The Wreckers" and "The Boatswain's Mate", and who by her example undoubtedly inspired many women to apply themselves to the difficult art of composition. Of the present generation two British women composers at least have succeeded in making a name for themselves—Elizabeth Lutyens and Elizabeth Maconchy. Miss Lutyens, who is now the wife of that well-known conductor and promoter of contemporary music, Edward Clark, was particularly active during the war and produced a number of works which undoubtedly add to her already growing reputation as a composer with a style of her own and a very definite musical personality. It so happened that her "Three Pieces for Orchestra" were played at a Promenade Concert conducted by the late Sir Henry Wood on the night when the Germans opened their air offensive against London. The following year she was evacuated with her children to the country, where in the face of all sorts of difficulties and in the intervals of looking after her husband

and family she managed nevertheless to compose a number of works, one of which, the " Concerto for Nine Instruments ", was accepted by the English Jury of the I.S.C.M. in 1940 and has been performed both in London and in the U.S.A. Among other recent works from her pen are the " Nine Bagatelles " for 'cello and piano; a Concerto for Clarinet, Saxophone, Piano and String Orchestra; " Five Intermezzi " for piano solo, and " Three Salutes to the United Nations ". Since returning to London Miss Lutyens has written " Three Symphonic Preludes " for orchestra, performed at the Festival of the I.S.C.M. in London in July 1946; an overture, " Proud City " (in honour of London); a Concerto for Bassoon and String Orchestra; some film music; and a " Suite Gauloise ", the first movement of which was commissioned by the French Government for inclusion in an album of piano pieces by British composers entitled " Hommage à la France ". Mention should also be made of a striking Sonata for Solo Viola which had its first performance at a concert organised by the Society for the Promotion of New Music.

Elizabeth Maconchy (b. 1907) is, like Miss Lutyens, a modernist and cultivates a style that has been described by a contemporary critic as " vigorous and thoughtful, sometimes impassioned but rarely lyrical ". Her music has on several occasions found favour with the Juries of the I.S.C.M. and several of her works have been performed on the Continent, notably at Brussels, Warsaw, Prague, Budapest and Cracow. Of Irish parentage, but largely trained and mostly resident in England, Elizabeth Maconchy started to compose at the age of six. She has written four String Quartets, an Oboe Quintet, a Concerto for Viola and Orchestra, and a Piano Concerto which was performed in Prague in 1930.

When war broke out Miss Maconchy was living in Southern England, and while the Battle of Britain was proceeding overhead she wrote her ballet " Puck Fair ", which was produced in Dublin at the Gaiety Theatre the same year (1940). Her " Dialogue for Piano and Orchestra " was to have had its first performance at a Promenade Concert the same year, but owing to air raids the concerts had to be discontinued. However, the work was given two years later under the late Sir Henry Wood, with Clifford Curzon as the soloist. More recent works from her pen include: String Quartet

No. 4 (broadcast by the B.B.C. in their Home and Foreign Services); a set of Variations for Orchestra, commissioned by the B.B.C. and broadcast in the special programmes to celebrate the seventieth birthday of Vaughan Williams; Variations for String Orchestra (broadcast from Dublin in July 1945); a Sonata for Violin and Piano (performed at a concert of the London Contemporary Music Society in 1945); and several songs and smaller works. To this period also belongs a choral work, for women's voices, entitled " Stalingrad ", which has been performed in London and at Music Festivals in the provinces. Miss Maconchy's Concertino for Clarinet and Strings was selected for performance at I.S.C.M. Festival at Copenhagen in June 1947.

It is time now to close this brief survey of the activities and achievements of British musicians during the war. Enough has perhaps been said to provide evidence that, in spite of the material dangers and difficulties to which this country was exposed during six long years, spiritual and artistic values were never lost sight of or allowed to be submerged in the heat and dust of the struggle. Musically, Britain has won her spurs and can now face the future with confidence. Gone are the days when it was possible for foreign nations to refer to her as " the land without music ". It was never true, and never less so than today.

APPENDIX

GRAMOPHONE RECORDS

* Denotes a special recording under the auspices of the British Council.

Arnold Bax

"A Hill Tune"; "A Mountain Mood". Harriet Cohen (Pianoforte). Col. DX.1109.

"Hardanger" (Sonata for Two Pianos). Ethel Bartlett and Rae Robertson (Pianofortes). N.G.S. 156-8.

"Tintagel"; "Mediterranean". New Symphony Orchestra conducted by Eugene Goossens. H.M.V. C.1619-20.

Oboe Quintet. Leon Goossens (Oboe) and the International String Quartet. N.G.S. 76-7.

Overture to a Picaresque Comedy. London Philharmonic Orchestra conducted by Sir Hamilton Harty. Col. LX.394.

Sonata for Viola and Harp. Watson Forbes (Viola) and Maria Korchinska (Harp). Decca K.941-3.

String Quartet in G Major No. 1. Marie Wilson String Quartet. N.G.S. 153-5.

String Quartet in G Major No. 1. The Griller Quartet. Decca K.1009-12.

Symphony No. 3.* Hallé Orchestra conducted by John Barbirolli. H.M.V. C.3380-5 (Non-Automatic). H.M.V. C. 7593-8 (Automatic).

English Music Society, Vol. 2:

Sonata for Viola and Piano; Nonett for String Quartet, with Bass, Flute, Clarinet, Oboe and Harp; Mater Ora Filium. William Primrose (Viola), Harriet Cohen (Pianoforte), Griller String Quartet, Leon Goossens (Oboe), Frederick Thurston (Clarinet), Jos. Slater (Flute), Victor Watson (Bass), Maria Korchinska (Harp), B.B.C. Chorus conducted by Leslie Woodgate. Col. ROX.179-85 (Non-Automatic). Col. ROX.8039-45 (Automatic).

"I Heard a Piper Piping"; "Linden Lea" (Vaughan Williams). Astra Desmond (Contralto) and Gerald Moore (Pianoforte). Decca M.522.

Arthur Bliss

Clarinet Quintet; Polonaise. Frederick Thurston (Clarinet) and Griller String Quartet. Decca K.780-3.

Concerto for Pianoforte and Orchestra.* Solomon (Pianoforte) and Liverpool Philharmonic Orchestra conducted by Sir Adrian Boult.

H.M.V. C.3348-52 (Non-Automatic). H.M.V. C.7583-7 (Automatic).

Film Music ("Things to Come"). London Symphony Orchestra. DECCA K.810-11 and K.817.

Music for Strings. B.B.C. Symphony Orchestra conducted by Sir Adrian Boult. H.M.V. DB.3257-9 (Non-Automatic). H.M.V. DB.8342-4 (Automatic).

Quartet in B Flat. Griller String Quartet. DECCA K.1091-4.

Sonata for Viola and Piano. Watson Forbes (Viola) and Myers Foggin (Pianoforte). DECCA X.233-5.

"Baraza" (Incidental music from the film "Men of Two Worlds"). Eileen Joyce (Pianoforte) and the National Symphony Orchestra and Male Chorus conducted by Muir Mathieson. DECCA K.1174.

The Phoenix March* (in honour of France). Philharmonia Orchestra conducted by Constant Lambert. H.M.V. C.3518.

"Miracle in the Gorbals"—Ballet Suite. Royal Opera House Orchestra, Covent Garden, conducted by Constant Lambert. COL. DX.1260-61.

Benjamin Britten

Introduction and Rondo alla Burlesca for Two Pianos, Opus 23, No. 1. Clifford Curzon and Benjamin Britten. DECCA K.1117.

Mazurka Elegiaca for Two Pianos, Opus 23, No. 2. Clifford Curzon and Benjamin Britten. DECCA K.1118.

"Le Roi s'en va-t-en chasse"; "La Belle est au Jardin d'Amour" (French Folk Songs). Sophie Wyss (Soprano) and Benjamin Britten (Pianoforte). DECCA M.568.

Seven Sonnets of Michelangelo, Nos. XXX, XVI and XXXI (in Italian). Peter Pears (Tenor) and Benjamin Britten (Pianoforte). H.M.V. B.9302 and H.M.V. C.3312.

Simple Symphony. Boyd Neel String Orchestra conducted by Boyd Neel. DECCA X.245-7.

Variations on a Theme of Frank Bridge. Boyd Neel String Orchestra conducted by Boyd Neel. DECCA X.226-8.

Serenade for Tenor, Horn and Strings. Peter Pears (Tenor), Dennis Brain (Horn) and the Boyd Neel String Orchestra conducted by Benjamin Britten. DECCA K.1151-3 (Non-Automatic). DECCA AK.1151-3 (Automatic).

A Ceremony of Carols. The Morriston Boys' Choir with Maria Korchinska (Harp). Choir Master: Ivor Sims. DECCA K.1155-7 (Non-Automatic). DECCA AK.1155-7 (Automatic).

Hymn to St. Cecilia, Opus 27; "This have I done", Opus 34 (Holst). Fleet Street Choir conducted by T. B. Lawrence. DECCA K.1088-9.

Folk Songs: "The Sally Gardens", "Little Sir William" and "Oliver Cromwell". Peter Pears (Tenor) and Benjamin Britten (Pianoforte). DECCA M.555.

John Ireland

Concerto in E Flat for Pianoforte and Orchestra. Eileen Joyce (Pianoforte) and the Hallé Orchestra conducted by Leslie Heward. COL. DX.1072-4 (Non-Automatic). COL. DX.8178-80 (Automatic).

Concertino Pastorale; Downland Suite (Minuet). Boyd Neel String Orchestra conducted by Boyd Neel. DECCA X.253-5.

Phantasie Trio in A Minor; Holy Boy. Grinke Trio. DECCA K.899-900.

Trio No. 3 in E. Grinke Trio. DECCA X.242-4.

London Overture. Liverpool Philharmonic Orchestra conducted by Sir Malcolm Sargent. COL. DX.1155-6.

"Sea Fever"; "The Road to the Isles" (Kennedy-Fraser). Robert Irwin (Baritone). H.M.V. B.9073.

"Sea Fever"; "Absent" (Metcalfe). Paul Robeson (Bass). H.M.V. B.9257.

Constant Lambert

Horoscope—Ballet Suite. Liverpool Philharmonic Orchestra conducted by Constant Lambert. COL. DX.1196-7.

E. J. Moeran

Symphony in G Minor.* The Hallé Orchestra conducted by Leslie Heward. H.M.V. C.3319-24 (Non-Automatic). H.M.V. C.7566-71 (Automatic).

Alan Rawsthorne

"Street Corner" Overture.* Philharmonia Orchestra conducted by Constant Lambert. H.M.V. C.3502.

Bagatelles for Piano. Four (1938). Denis Matthews. H.M.V. C.3324.

Ralph Vaughan Williams

Concerto Accademico (Concerto in D minor for Violin and String Orchestra). Frederick Grinke (Violin) and Boyd Neel String Orchestra conducted by Boyd Neel. DECCA X.248-9.

English Folk Songs (Suite). Columbia Broadcasting Symphony Orchestra. COL. DB.1930-31.

Greensleeves Fantasia. Hallé Orchestra conducted by Sir Malcolm Sargent. COL. DX.1087.

Fantasia on a Theme by Thomas Tallis. B.B.C. Symphony Orchestra conducted by Sir Adrian Boult. H.M.V. DB.3958-9.

" The Lark Ascending "; " Eventide ". Frederick Grinke (Violin) and Boyd Neel Orchestra conducted by Boyd Neel. Decca X.259-60.

" Serenade to Music." B.B.C. Orchestra with Sixteen Famous Soloists conducted by Sir Henry Wood. Col. LX.757-8.

Symphony in F Minor (No. 4.). B.B.C. Symphony Orchestra conducted by Dr. Ralph Vaughan Williams. H.M.V. DB.3367-70 (Non-Automatic). H.M.V. DB.8406-9 (Automatic).

Symphony in D Major* (No. 5). Hallé Orchestra conducted by John Barbirolli. H.M.V. C.3388-92 (Non-Automatic). H.M.V. C.7599-7603 (Automatic).

" The Wasps " Overture; Fantasia on " Greensleeves " (Vaughan Williams). Queen's Hall Orchestra conducted by Sir Henry Wood. Decca K.821-2.

" A London Symphony." Queen's Hall Orchestra conducted by Sir Henry Wood. Decca X.114-18.

" The Wasps " Overture. Hallé Orchestra conducted by Sir Malcolm Sargent. Col. DX. 1088.

" Linden Lea "; " I Heard a Piper Piping " (Bax). Astra Desmond (Contralto) and Gerald Moore (Pianoforte). Decca M.522.

Job—A Masque for Dancing. B.B.C. Symphony Orchestra conducted by Sir Adrian Boult. H.M.V. DB.6289-94 (Non-Automatic). H.M.V. DB.9024-8 (Automatic).

" Silent Noon "; " Tell me Ye Flowerets " (Stanford). David Lloyd (Tenor). Col. DB.2159.

William Walton

" Belshazzar's Feast."* Liverpool Philharmonic Orchestra and Brass Bands, Dennis Noble (Baritone) and the Huddersfield Choir conducted by Dr. William Walton. H.M.V. C.3330-34 (Non-Automatic). H.M.V. C.7572-6 (Automatic).

Concerto for Viola and Orchestra. Frederick Riddle (Viola) and the London Symphony Orchestra conducted by Dr. William Walton. Decca X.199-201.

Concerto for Violin and Orchestra. Jascha Heifetz (Violin) and Cincinnati Symphony Orchestra conducted by Eugene Goossens. H.M.V. DB.5953-5 (Non-Automatic). H.M.V. DB.8911-13 (Automatic).

" Crown Imperial "—Coronation March, 1937. B.B.C. Symphony Orchestra with Berkeley Mason (Organ) conducted by Sir Adrian Boult. H.M.V. DB.3164.

" Façade " Suite No. 1. London Philharmonic Orchestra conducted by Dr. William Walton. H.M.V. C.2836-7.

" Façade " Suite No. 2; Siesta. London Philharmonic Orchestra conducted by Dr. William Walton. H.M.V. C.3042.

Piano Quartet. Reginald Paul Piano Quartet. DECCA X.2238-41.

" Portsmouth Point " Overture. B.B.C. Symphony Orchestra conducted by Sir Adrian Boult. H.M.V. DA.1540.

Prelude and " Spitfire " Fugue. Hallé Orchestra conducted by Dr. William Walton. H.M.V. C.3359.

" Scapino "—A Comedy Overture. Chicago Symphony Orchestra. COLUMBIA LX. 931.

Symphony in B Flat Minor. London Symphony Orchestra conducted by Sir Hamilton Harty. DECCA X.108-13.

" Wise Virgins " Ballet Suite. Sadler's Wells Orchestra conducted by Dr. William Walton. H.M.V. C.3178-9.

" Sinfonia Concertante "; " Death of Falstaff "; " Touch her Lips ". Phyllis Sellick (Pianoforte) and City of Birmingham Orchestra conducted by Dr. William Walton (" Sinfonia Concertante "). Philharmonia Orchestra conducted by Dr. William Walton (" Death of Falstaff " and " Touch her Lips "). H.M.V. C.3478-80 (Non-Automatic). H.M.V. C.7635-7 (Automatic).

" Where does the uttered music go? " B.B.C. Chorus conducted by Leslie Woodgate. H.M.V. C.3503.

Viola Concerto. William Primrose (Viola) and the Philharmonia Orchestra conducted by Dr. William Walton. H.M.V. DB.6309-11. (Non-Automatic). H.M.V. DB.9036-8 (Automatic).

PAINTING SINCE 1939

ROBIN IRONSIDE

PAINTING SINCE 1939

IN THIS critical study of painting in Britain since 1939, Mr. Ironside interprets the significant trends of the war years, and surveys the work of Duncan Grant, Stanley Spencer, Paul Nash, Ben Nicholson, John Piper, Graham Sutherland, Henry Moore, Victor Pasmore and other contemporary artists. The interest of the essay is not confined to this period, however; it derives permanent value from its relation of the most advanced modern work to the influence of great artists of the past and to certain enduring traits of British art.

Mr. Robin Ironside is himself an artist of distinction and his pictures have been acquired for the Tate Gallery, The Contemporary Art Society and other collections. He is well known also as a critic, and is a contributor to *Horizon* and other periodicals.

CONTENTS

The opinions expressed in this book are the author's, and not necessarily those of the British Council

ILLUSTRATIONS

Victor Pasmore, *The Gardens of Hammersmith* (1944), $36'' \times 24''$, oil; owned by Hugo Pitman, Esq.

Francis Bacon, *Painting*, $77'' \times 51''$, oil ; owned by the Lefevre Gallery, London

Robert Colquhoun, *Woman with Folded Arms* (1945), $36'' \times 24''$, oil; owned by the Lefevre Gallery, London

Henry Moore, *Draped Figures in Shelter* (1941), $22'' \times 12\frac{1}{2}''$, water-colour and pen; owned by Julian Huxley, Esq.

Between pages 156 and 157

David Jones, *Thorn Cup* (1932), $30\frac{1}{8}'' \times 22''$, water-colour and pencil; owned by Miss Helen Sutherland

David Jones, *Guinevere* (1940), $24\frac{1}{2}'' \times 19\frac{1}{2}''$, ink and water-colour; owned by the Tate Gallery

Lucien Freud, *Drawing of an Owl* (1945)

Paul Nash, *Sunflower and Sun* (1943), $19\frac{1}{2}'' \times 21\frac{1}{2}''$, oil; owned by The Contemporary Art Society

Between pages 164 and 165

Edward Burra, *Soldiers* (1942), $41\frac{1}{2}'' \times 81\frac{1}{2}''$, water-colour; owned by the Tate Gallery

Henry Moore, *Draped Standing Figures* (1946), $22'' \times 15''$, chalk and water-colour; collection of Viscount Moore

Albert Richards, *Withdrawing from the Battery* (1944), $21\frac{1}{4}'' \times 20\frac{3}{4}''$, water-colour; owned by the Tate Gallery

Graham Sutherland, *Small Boulder* (1940), $9\frac{3}{8}'' \times 5\frac{1}{4}''$, gouache; owned by the Hon. Edward Sackville-West

Between pages 172 and 173

Henry Moore, *Seated Figure and Pointed Forms* (1940), 17″ × 10″, chalk and water-colour; owned by Miss Lee Miller

Ben Nicholson, *Still Life*, 1945, 32⅝″ × 23¾″, oil; owned by the Tate Gallery

Stanley Spencer, *Christ in the Wilderness—the Scorpions* (1939), 21½″ × 21½″, oil; owned by J. L. Behrend, Esq.

Victor Pasmore, *Everlasting Flowers* (1941), 18″ × 24″, oil; owned by Lady Herbert

John Piper, *Gordale Scar* (1943), 30″ × 25″, oil; owned by Sir Kenneth Clark

Ceri Richards, *Blossoms*, 20″ × 24″, oil; owned by the Tate Gallery

Frances Hodgkins, *Wings Over Water*, 36″ × 25″, oil; owned by Temple Newsam House, Leeds

John Craxton, *Alderholt Mill, Dorset* (1944), 18″ × 23½″; owned by Peter Watson, Esq.

Between pages 180 and 181

Grateful acknowledgment for permission to reproduce the plates is made to the artists and owners

---

The colour plates are reproduced by kind permission of Penguin Books Ltd. (Modern Painters' series)

PAINTING SINCE 1939

I. GENERAL CHARACTER OF BRITISH PAINTING

It has usually been at the ultimate bidding of more or less unprofessional sentiment that British painters have produced their most affecting works. The truth may be that all great art is the fruit of an original impulse transcending the mere professional, not to say the vocational, interest—that the significance, for the greatest painters, of the practice of painting is trifling in relation to the languors or upheavals of the mind of which their pictures are but the key. This point, however, is possibly as controversial as it is attractive, and the unprofessional mainspring of the best British painting is noted here not as a recommendation, but as a distinguishing feature; there is no need to emphasise the fact that it is not one that of necessity contributes to excellence. Nor can the merits of those pictures be intelligently denied whose beauty resides, to the exclusion of all else, in the nice intricacies or meditated simplifications of handling and composition. But painting of such a rigorously sensuous kind, obedient to a fine, functional stringency, has been an infrequent and unproductive occurrence in the history of British art. It is a history that chiefly records the achievements of a landscape school, yet the configuration of the soil, the contours of the woods, the inexhaustible variety of the English light, have never been successfully used as the mere pretext for a telling assembly of colours or interplay of projections and recessions. We do indeed delight in Turner's unrivalled skill, but the quintessence of his art is somewhere hidden in his love for nature as a symbolic mirror of human destinies; the inevitable setting of the sun may well have been, for him, an emblem of the *Fallacies of Hope*—the title of his reputedly long poem of which only a few unequal fragments are now extant; and his masterpieces are imperfectly understood by those who disregard the lofty reflections that recurringly incited his genius upon the transience of empires, the spaciousness of dawns or the fury of the elements. The chequered fabric of Constable's pictures, their deep undertones overlaid with variegated passages of crumbling impasto and strewn with particles of white light, might suffice to perpetuate his fame, but the painter was more deeply concerned to convey the spiritual force of " one impulse from a vernal wood " than with any creative potentialities inherent in the art he practised. The bucolic landscape of Gainsborough was not less the manifestation of sentiments that might have been expressed by other means, of sentiments that could not, in their essence, be considered the peculiar province of a painter. There has been no British master such—to quote the obvious examples—as Manet or Velasquez whose visual responses were so little either impeded or enriched by the intrusion of motives irrelevant to the inventive exploitation of their medium. The genius of these two painters may be incautiously defined within such narrow limits, but it is evident that the pleasure they communicate arises in great part from the material substance of their works, that their art would best be expounded in the manner of Fromentin, in the technical phraseology of the studio. We may legitimately emphasise the heterogeneous inspiration of such brilliant practitioners as Constable and Turner; when we examine the inferior standards of execution of Blake and his followers or of the young Rossetti, there is no need to stress how little the imaginative force of their work is served by professional acumen. An artist of such undisputed genius and such indifferent skill as Blake, for whom the visible world hardly existed, has few parallels among continental painters. He may have few equals among British artists, but the combination of an unpenetrating eye or inexpert hand with a genuine power of artistic conception is a characteristic one in the history of the little Masters of British painting, whether we cite the eighteenth-century pastoralism of John Cozens (1752–1799), the mythological evocations of Edward Calvert (1799–1883) or the poetic illustrations of the less pretentious Victorian Romantics. The best British painting relies, for its final justification, upon an amateur stimulus, that is to say, upon a stimulus that may be ethical, poetic or philosophic but not simply plastic, not a stimulus transmitted by any pure, inflexible aesthetic perception of the external world.

II. THE INFLUENCE OF ROGER FRY

The fertility of such exotic impulses may be asserted with peculiar relevance today. During the first two decades of the twentieth century and for some years previously, British painting was subject to tendencies and theories that renounced as an intrusion the presence in pictures of values other than those of rhythm, texture, colour and, above all, of form and composition. At present, the most inspired manifestations of the modern school are eloquent of thoughts and feeling for which, indeed, such values constitute the indispensable terminology; but this linguistic function is rarely exceeded and we may feel that the painter's conceptions are alive irrespective of any problem of materialisation, that they do not at first subsist in any inherent or inevitable relation to the visual terms in which they are ultimately set forth. The idea of an exclusive and all-sufficing beauty in plastic values still persists; but its practical application, which never produced outstanding results, is now increasingly neglected and, with few exceptions, fruitlessly attempted. That the idea should survive as part of a culture so ill-conditioned to uncompromising theories is due not only to the genuine but narrow ray of light that it shed upon the indefinite nature of fine art, but more, perhaps than to anything else, to the far-reaching influence of the teachings of Roger Fry. The mixed emotional under currents of recent British painting, nourished as they have been by the springs of continental surrealism and by the dews and storms of English Romantic art in the early nineteenth century, are also the signs of a strong natural reaction against the aesthetic purism of Fry's critical doctrines. For him, the contrast in a picture of recession and projection, the interplay of planes, the progression of form sequences composed, to use his own words, " a music and a melody ", and their coalescence into an ordered unity had the power to satisfy and elate him in much the same way as the demonstration of a complex mathematical equation may be exhilarating to a mathematician. He was rarely prompted, and probably never tempted, to seek the ultimate significance of a picture beyond the workings of these—in art—imponderable factors. He felt that " the one constant and unchanging emotion before works of art had to do always with the contemplation of form and that this was more profound and significant spiritually than any of the emotions which had to do with life ". This critical attitude was expertly applied in Fry's enthusiastic appreciations of French painting of the end of the nineteenth and the beginning of the twentieth centuries; it was largely through his agency that the art of Cézanne, Gauguin, Van Gogh and of the twentieth-century Paris School was introduced to the artists and the public in Great Britain, over whom it acquired and has, till recently, continued to exercise the same pervasive influence that it exerted elsewhere. It is unnecessary to regret and it would have been vain to resist the hegemony of a school whose authority was at first exclusively derived from the vigour of its genius. But the prestige of the *Fauves* and their dependants outlasted, in London, the decline of their influence —and powers—on the continent; and it was unfortunate that Fry's rousing analyses of the art of the illustrious predecessors of *Fauvisme* should have directed attention upon the patient manipulation of volumes that was a feature of Cézanne's method rather than upon the rich, repining vision of a primitive elysium that flowed from Gauguin's very essence. The way was thus paved for the emulation of the art of Matisse, Derain, Vlaminck—rather than that of Chagall, Rouault or Chirico to which the native temper might have been more easily attuned.

The widespread admission of the overriding importance of plastic values may have proved a seasonable if transitory discipline; it confined the legitimate concern of the painter to the elementary and inalienable obligation of his art, to the studied arrangement of shapes and colours. But there are painters working today who too unreservedly espoused the cause, whose gifts were contracted rather than purified by the controls it imposed; their art has withered, and their brief celebrity evaporated with the vitality of the ideas that were its principal support. Only a few of those who have resisted the infection of less sterilised ideals have still the power to delight or excite us, and their resistance has been due much less to the depth of their conviction than the necessity of their personality. Duncan Grant and Matthew Smith are at once their most lively and venerable representatives. Duncan Grant

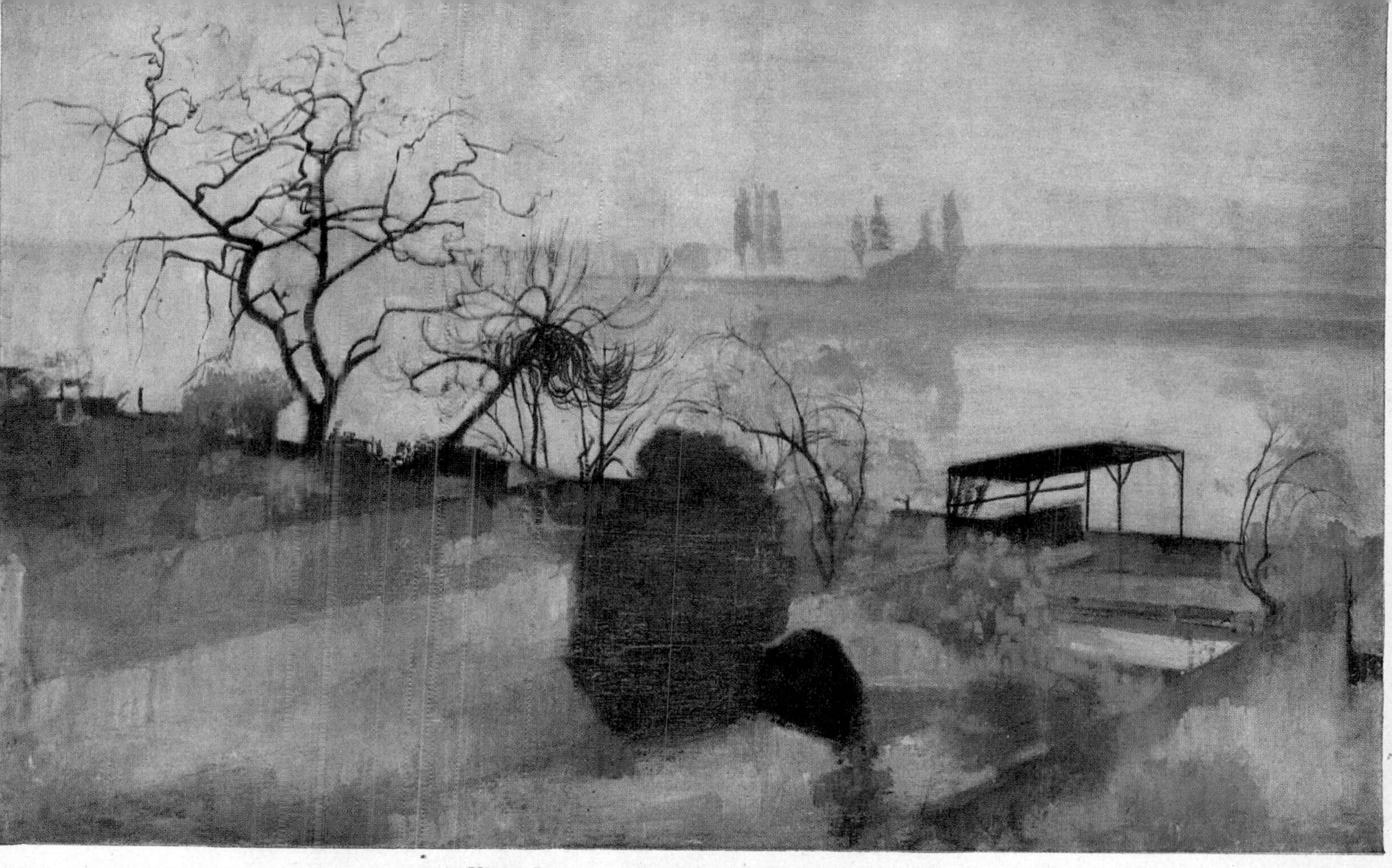

Victor Pasmore, *The Gardens of Hammersmith* (1944)

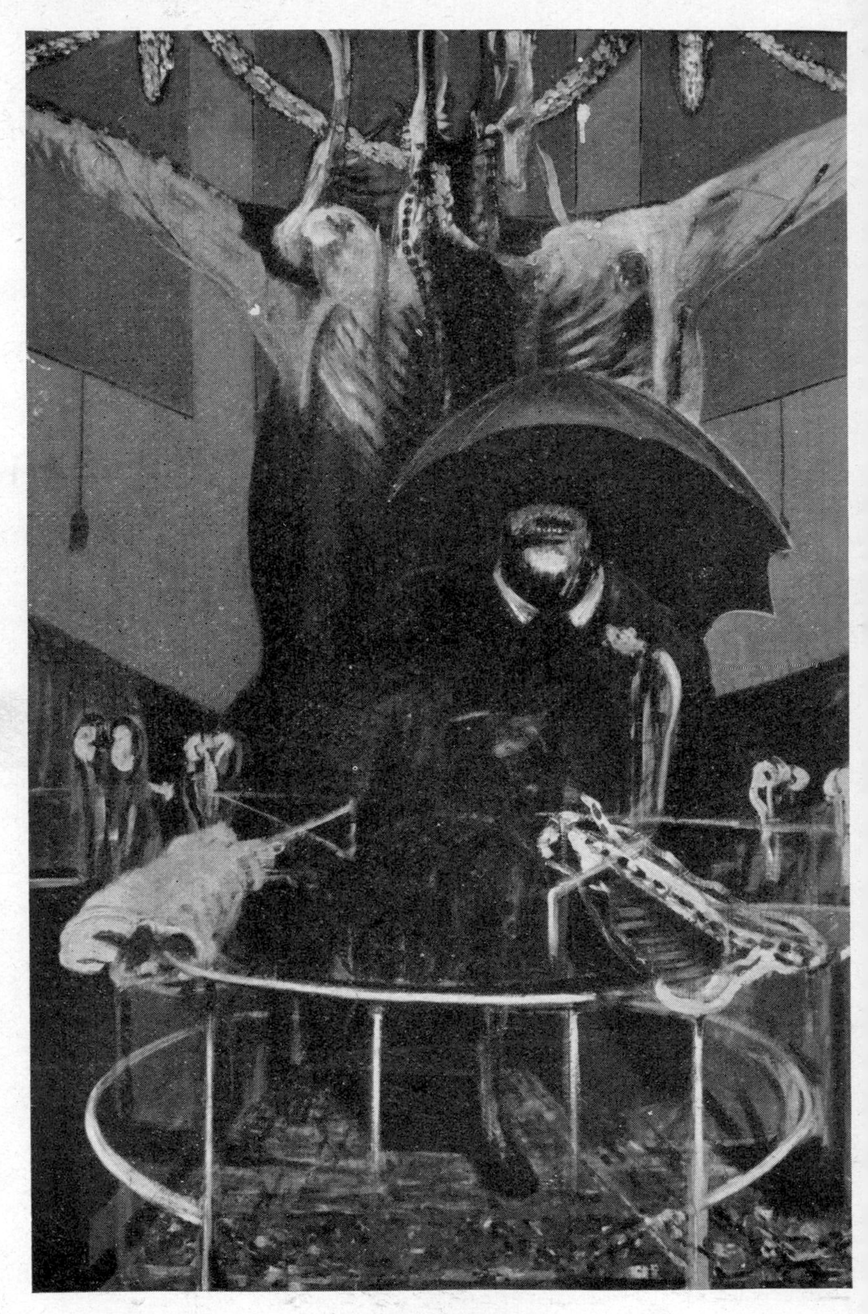

Francis Bacon, *Painting*

Robert Colquhoun, *Woman with Folded Arms* (1945)

Henry Moore, *Draped Figures in Shelter* (1941)

was closely associated with Roger Fry and he may have developed the Cézannesque traits in his art from an intellectual submission to the critic's spell-binding advocacy of Cézanne's genius. His landscapes and still-lifes sometimes betray a somewhat ponderous endeavour to realise the formal plenitude of the motif, to balance the disposition of the various masses in his composition, an endeavour which has never seemed in adequate accord with the elegant, sometimes blithe personality revealed in his most successful work. It is as the manifestation of an acute decorative sensibility rather than of any power of monumental composition in depth that his art is in instinctive harmony with certain phases of the Paris School; and as such, also, its valid concern is only with its own rhythms and modulations. His main performance as a decorative painter dates from before the war, but his *Girl at the Piano*, painted in 1940 and acquired by the Tate Gallery, is a richly woven, diapered fabric; encumbered as it may seem to be in parts by an unprofitable solidity of treatment, it suggests, in its warm polychromy, compositions on the same theme by Matisse. To associate the art of Matthew Smith with that of Duncan Grant may seem unwarrantable to those who are familiar with their styles. The painting of the former is so clearly the product of temperament rather than of sensibility or forethought. Yet both are indebted to the same French influences and both profess an art that is autonomous, an art of which the forms and colours refer only to one another. Matthew Smith was directly inspired by the *Fauves*; the sensuous violence of his colour sense was liberated by contact with their art. He subsequently abandoned the somewhat shocking contrasts of hot and cold colour cultivated by *Fauvisme* in its first unbridled moments, but it seems likely that, in some instances, the raw splendour of his earlier works may survive the richer effulgence of his mature manner, though this indeed shows no signs of a diminishing light. His talent has continued throughout the war to produce mounting, almost superfluous, proof of its opulence, some of his recent still-lifes revealing depths of colour that he had not hitherto sounded. Smith is also a painter of nudes, landscapes and occasional portraits. But whatever the inducements and interests may be that finally decide the choice of his theme, an admirer of his painting would not admit their direct artistic relevance; and whatever the decipherable subject of his pictures, whether it is a female torso or a basket of peaches, our lasting impression, if it is still of fruit, flowers or flesh, is an impression of these phenomena not as a reality or as a dream, but as the emblazoned motif, simply, of some vast, glowing arras or carpet that the artist offers, in selected pieces, for our inspection. His art, like that of Duncan Grant, appears unconscious, and is at least disrespectful, of its iconographical element. The work of both painters is historically related to the aspirations of the beginning of the century, and preserves its circumscribed appeal—and may have confirmed its repute—amid the diffuse, figurative currents of thought and sensation that have animated more recent developments.

III. EMERGENCE OF THE NEO-ROMANTIC SPIRIT

It is the broad truth that British painting since 1939 has accomplished, or almost accomplished, the revival of a liberal conception of the art as a creative instrument for the communication, not simply of those specialised emotions that the felicitous arrangement of forms and colours may arouse in us, but also for the communication by imagery, whether the imaginative vision be naturalistic or not, of any emotion whatever. But the convenience—not to say, the validity—of generalised truths of this nature depends in most cases upon a due consideration of the modifications or exceptions to which all generalisations are subject. It would be a mistake to infer that the ideas propagated by Roger Fry and their powerful justification by examples from French painting ever exercised an exclusive influence, or that more mixed, more romantic tendencies than would have been suffered under that restrictive dispensation alone were not manifest, in whatever comparative isolation, prior to 1939.

No account of modern British painting could ignore the peculiar art of Stanley Spencer; though his finest work dates unquestionably from before 1921, or even, some might say, from before the first

World War, his productive vigour has continued unabated to this moment. It must be admitted that such a picture as his *Apple Gatherers*, painted in 1912, reveals a momentary submission to the ideal that was then awakening with Fry's encouragement, of the independence of plastic values; but the totality of his achievement derives its character from motives entirely alien to such a limited objective. His art has been successively possessed by religious and sexual preoccupations, and the flow of landscapes and flower-pieces that has relieved the oppression of his violent dealings with these major emotional themes owes the force of its current to the painter's rooted affection for the commons and blossoms of his native village rather than to any unrelated concern with forms and colours. Spencer's style with its idiosyncratic distortions of the human figure bears some resemblance to that of the youthful Pre-Raphaelites and reflects, not less faintly than did theirs, the illustrious example of the early Florentine painters. It is a style the peculiarity of which has not diminished with the years; it has exerted no effect upon the painters whose reputations developed during the recent war; and Spencer remains an artist whose imaginative powers have revolved locally (though they were doubtless in part released by the influx of foreign influences during the first decade of the century) and whose unique position today may be ascribed to the combination provided by his art of a pronounced modernity of conception with a method of handling too reminiscent of the past to provoke emulation. His most affecting achievement of recent years is the series of small panels (1939) on the theme of Christ in the wilderness; the studied *naïveté* with which these interpret their subject contrives to produce a grotesque but not an offensive impression. On the other hand, the large compositions illustrating the work of shipyards, which were carried out for the War Artists Advisory Committee and are the artist's most spectacular recent productions, display a vigour and a virtuosity which, though they command our respect, have been exercised perhaps with less inspiration, and certainly with less decorative sense, than are evident in his previous undertakings on a similar scale. Spencer's art maintains its hardiness, but it has not yet surpassed the magic level of devotional intensity that it reached, for example, in the *Nativity* painted in 1912.

Spencer was, without doubt, in the inter-war years, the artist whose work was most significantly at variance with the prevalent ideal. But our conception of the effective extent of this ideal requires further modification; it had no sooner been intellectually accepted by the community of serious artists than—as we may, in retrospect, affirm—a sentimental reaction was perceptibly set in motion. Such subtle, pacific interpenetrations of conflicting attitudes may constitute a commonplace for the student of art history; their perpetual recurrence can be illustrated—to take a clear and familiar instance—by recalling how positively the specific qualities of French Revolutionary and Imperial art were moulded by that of the Louis-Seize period, or by an examination of the more complex but still not abstruse notion that origins of the Baroque style may be discoverable in the flamboyancy of fifteenth-century Gothic art. It should not be impossible to unravel these processes in the modest instance with which we are here concerned. But it is questionable whether such remote and impersonal consideration might not be improperly applied in detail to the work of living artists. We may at least assert that the unhampered imaginative and emotional conception of the art of painting that distinguishes what is best in British art at this moment and may be qualified, for reasons of convenience, as "neo-romantic", includes, among its most spontaneous adherents, painters whose previous allegiance to narrower standards, genuine as it was, might have been seen to be a tenuous bond.

David Jones became temporarily interested, when a pupil at the Westminster Art School *circa* 1919, in the work of those London painters in whom the example of Parisian art—and the effect of the theories that were derived from it—were most unquestioningly evident. His own painting was influenced to a limited extent by their practices; and he has relied exclusively, in some of his landscapes and still-lifes, upon a gift for linear pattern and upon the extreme delicacy of his colour sense. He has, however, always drawn a more profound inspiration from his emotional responses to Christian, and particularly Celtic mythology. In his art, fancy, exquisitely tuned, semi-religious, ultimately triumphs over discipline. The elaborate fragility of his water-colour technique has become increasingly at the mercy of his fantastic apprehension of a pervading metamorphosis and mutability in the world, an apprehension that has led him to multiply the details in his pictures until, in his most complicated works which are always his finest, the host of accessories seem to flutter together, to transubstantiate themselves one into another, in accordance, one easily feels, with the same miraculous laws whereby bread and wine change their substance at Mass. After a period of inactivity shortly before the outbreak of war, this artist's fitful talent re-awoke, with intensified effect, in 1940, when he drew the two illustrations to the Arthurian legends, now in the Tate Gallery, *Guinevere* and *The Four Queens*. These pictures, the most advisedly poetic productions of his mature manner, amid whose faint tones there hovers a multitude of symbols gathered from the varying sources of the Arthurian cycle, may be described as a culmination of the painter's conceptions of landscape which had become more and more a perception, not of inherent qualities in nature, but of particular places as the fitting scenes of legendary events. The imaginative profusion of these latest drawings certainly owes something to the general emergence towards the end of the 'thirties of a romantic, anarchic view of the potentialities of fine art.

The later phases of the art of Paul Nash both reflected this view and hastened its propagation. Nash's youthful manner revealed the vision of a naturalist with stylistic tendencies towards ornamental abstraction. He subsequently yielded to the most restrictive of the systems emanating from French sources and it seemed for a moment as if the promise, the natural poetry, of some of his early landscapes was to be withered by the exclusive atmosphere of Constructivism. But the poet has been able to reassert himself in this forbidding climate. The primitive shapes, the ovoids and the rhomboids that the artist, under the influence of Constructivism, assembled without comment have become the fragments of a geography, of a natural zone, prehistoric in its configuration, but subject to the cyclical " history " of the seasons. The poetic action in Nash's recent pictures is the action of equinoxes, of the phases of the moon, of, in general, meteorological events. Nash had exhibited with the Surrealists before 1939; it is, however, since that date that his art, though in no doctrinaire surrealist sense, has most clearly displayed a hallucinatory quality. But there is nothing distempered in this quality. It has, when it is fully manifested, the beauty not of fever, but of frigidity. In his landscapes of the war years, the movements of the sun and the moon light up a planet sometimes of so ancient an aspect that the presence on it even of a dolmen would appear intrusive, and the giant aboriginal flowers which, in a still more recent group of works, have taken possession of the scene are characterised by the same exoticism, by the strangeness of flora in a primeval world. Perhaps the artist's most remarkable achievement in the immediate past is the series of sunsets in water-colour exhibited together in 1944. This medium, which Nash has always used with felicity, is peculiarly adapted to the expression of his cool, astringent vision. Whatever the redness of the sun in these water-colours, their general effect is of dew-like freshness; the hyperborean light which shines in them has been rendered with an impeccability, so to speak, of language, which yields the fine essence of the artist's current mood, a mood which is not always so unerringly active in his oil paintings.[1]

David Jones was an exhibitor with the Seven and Five Group. The historical interest of this society, founded shortly after the 1914–1918 war and now defunct, has never been sufficiently noticed. But a remarkable proportion of the painters whose work we value most today were at one time its members. It had a curious and unsuccessful beginning as an endeavour to co-ordinate any discoverable artistic tendencies that might plant the seeds in this country of Expressionism as it had developed on the continent. The constitution of the Group, however, allowed for the regular influx of new members, and, by the 'thirties, largely as a result of the advent of Ben Nicholson, a respect for abstract art had been introduced which engulfed the sentiments of the founders. Links were established with Arp and Mondrian in Paris and the exhibitions of the Group assumed a broadly non-representational character. But this it was found impossible to sustain at any worthy level. The progress of the Group as a whole (though it never had any real cultural homogeneity) illustrates the transience, which we

[1] Paul Nash died in July 1946.

have noticed in the specific instances of David Jones and Paul Nash, of the effect upon British painting of the plastic ideals pursued at the time with such rich results in France. Abstract art involves preoccupations too theoretic for widespread or faithful acceptance by a native culture that has at all times shown an almost instinctive preference for empirical philosophies. Even the work of the ultramontane abstractionist, Ben Nicholson, is marked, however he may attempt to resist it, by a recurrent capriciousness whose charm we miss in his more self-conscious and disciplined productions and whose suppression we are tempted to regard as wanton. The note of fancy was struck most sharply by Christopher Wood (1901–1930), whose art, in thrall as it was to the example of the French, preserved a positive quality of its own by the whimsicality of its variations upon stock European themes.

Frances Hodgkins, Winifred Nicholson and Ivon Hitchens, all of whom were members of the Seven and Five Group and whose debt to the non-representational developments of twentieth-century French painting was decisive, have become—or are now seen to be—painters whose lyrical interests were not to be subjected to any canon, who were incapable of separating their emotional reactions to nature from the formal constructions that they might (in search of harmonies and rhythms) choose to put upon it. Frances Hodgkins, certainly the most gifted of the numerous women painters at work in this country (the majority of whom follow at a distance the tracks of Dame Ethel Walker, the doyen of British Impressionism), is an artist who has always been sensitive to the possibilities, for the enrichment of her own personality, of the progress of styles on the continent. But the special qualities of her art, the mobility of its shapes and the subtle confusion of its colours, she has exploited, and continues to exploit, with a resistant verve that might be monotonous if it was less authentic. There is an evident and cultivated element of abstraction in her style, but, at her best, it serves rather than obscures a bucolic sentiment that is sometimes reminiscent of that of Chagall or, in her still-lifes, an associative affection for the assembled objects.[1]

The art of Winifred Nicholson, which, in all its stages, has been

[1] Frances Hodgkins died in May 1947.

affectingly if not openly feminine in the most charming and conventional sense, was for a moment influenced by a doctrinaire abstractionism of the kind to which others seek, apparently, to yield up altogether their talents. Her genuine merits, however, are of a more familiar nature. Her individual colour, distinguished by a combination of boldness and taste, can, without offence, be related to the discreet audacities of the best dress designers because it easily surpasses anything that dress designers at present achieve. It has become, furthermore, particularly in her recent pictures, the expression of what is almost a literary delight in everything that is fresh or immature in the appearances of nature. The animals that she paints have an undeveloped grace that might be described as providing a poetic counterpart to the somewhat vulgar realisations of Renée Sintenis on the same theme, not to mention those of the most approved of commercial purveyors of nursery art; and her spring flowers or snow-fields, while we may feel that they have been seen, however unconsciously, for children, are equally remote from the versions of such subjects with which the average intelligent parent has to be or is ready to be satisfied. Her art is of the kind with which we might wish to surround our children as our own comment upon their elegance and hardly caring whether they understood it or not. There can be little doubt that its almost irreproachable prettiness, when it is successful, owes much to the apparent earnestness with which its construction, its patterns and its colour harmonies appear to have been studied.

Ivon Hitchens was one of the earliest and most constant contributors to the exhibitions of the Seven and Five Group. His work as a student showed little or no promise of his subsequent development unless we may find in it evidence of a temperament unlikely to adapt itself for long to a purely decorative or intellectualised art. But it was contact with the Parisian School and notably, it may be supposed, with Matisse that was the principal factor in the evolution of his present style. Until shortly before the war his art, though based with deliberation upon natural motifs, made its principal appeal to the sensuous perceptions of the eye. It was variegated, bright, appearing to represent nothing, comparable, perhaps, to a clever and sensitive musical exercise. As early as 1937, however,

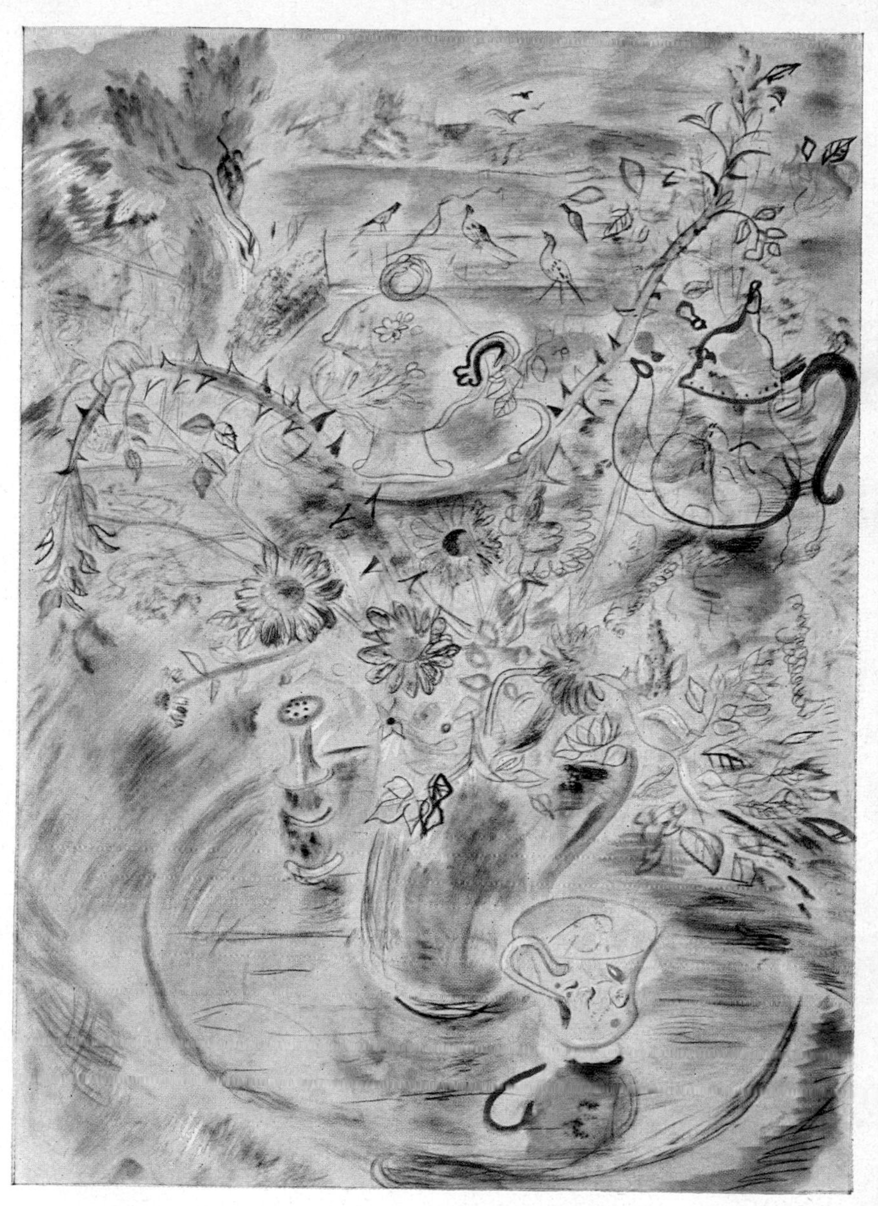

David Jones, *Thorn Cup* (1932)

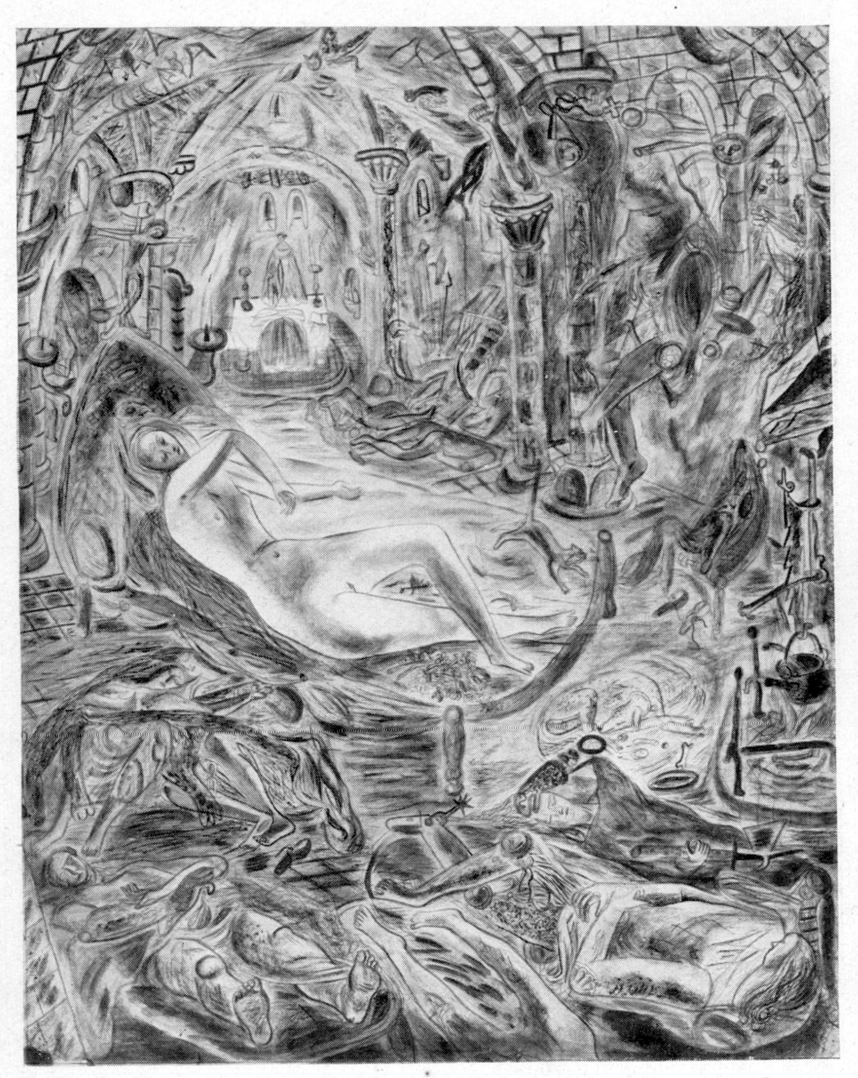

David Jones, *Guinevere* (1940)

Lucien Freud, *Drawing of an Owl* (1945)

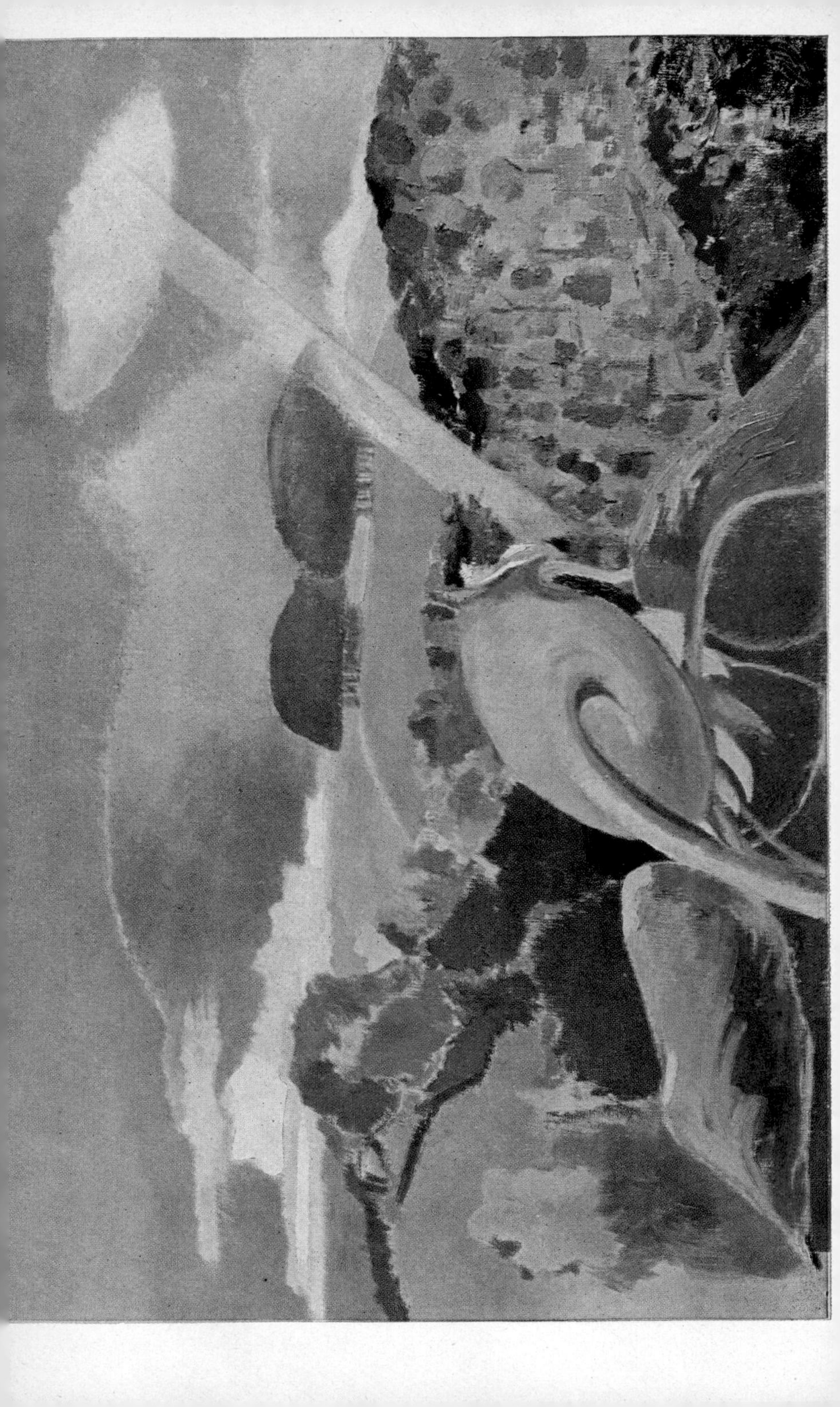

it became clear that coloured decoration, even of the vigorous, idiosyncratic type that he produced, was proving an inadequate vehicle of expression. Though Hitchens has continued to paint pictures in a bright key that seem to ask us for no more than a pleased acceptance—to continue the metaphor—of their harmonies, he has come to prefer and is most esteemed for autumnal colour schemes whose darker notes are not part of the pattern so much as hollows and vistas leading the spectator into recesses of the picture space. At the same time, the natural scenes whence the artist's vision is derived have become obtrusive. We clearly discern the groves, paths, pools and clusters of flowering shrubs which are among his favourite subjects and we perceive that they do not provide a pretext for a particular kind of artistic treatment, but that their natural charms govern the conception of the picture. Hitchens now appears as the special poet of those garden aspects of the scenery of the southern counties, the shadows of whose circumscribed woods are seasonally lit by rhododendrons and azaleas. The poetry is slight and the decorative abstractions in which it is wrapped would not, in themselves, have sustained indefinitely the artist's repute. But together they are the clear reflection of a sensitive personality, a reflection that in any contemporary exhibition reveals at first glance the pronounced individuality of its source.

To describe the art of Frances Hodgkins, Winifred Nicholson and Ivon Hitchens as neo-romantic would be taking gross advantage of a convenient label which may be reasonably used to cover the directing tendencies of contemporary British painting. These artists have, however (though they are in other ways very different), this leading trait in common, that their inspiration is lyrical; and it is a lyricism that overcame the formal disciplines of Parisian influence, a defeat which has left the painters apparently more at ease with their art. If we hesitate to link directly this revived lyricism with the broad imaginative currents that animate the contemporary school, it is nevertheless symptomatic of the development of our art during the last ten years, and, when we notice that, among the principal exponents of neo-romanticism, John Piper, Edward Burra and Henry Moore were also at various times members of the Seven and Five Group, we need no further warrant for calling special attention to this society as the local source not only of talent that has so far endured but of talent that has expanded and progressed. A close study of its history would be a general study of some of the best native reactions, adoptive, or resistant, to the non-representational ideals which largely dominated European art during the first decades of the present century.

The Group's last exhibition, held under the exclusive aegis of Ben Nicholson, was restricted to abstract works, a limitation which must have done much to ensure its final character. But the art of Ben Nicholson himself has continued to develop and shows signs at this moment of yet another reform of its peculiar features. Nicholson is the most convinced and consistent adherent of abstract painting in Great Britain. His early work, which includes expressive sea-scapes and coast scenes, revealed a painter endowed by nature with an esoteric technical ability, a gift that he has since cultivated in the pursuit of fine textures whose subtlety is exquisite when he shows his hand but whose precision at other times can only be compared to that of a machine. His abstractions are most effective when they are most fanciful, when they are composed in some formal but otherwise inconsequential relation to a known object, a cup, a boat or a flag. He exhibited shortly before the war a series of small Cornish landscapes; the remarkable craftsmanship they display, combined with a certain waywardness in their forms, suggests the perfection for which an inspired maker of toys might strive. In his first post-war exhibition he included a number of larger works—near abstractions—on related Cornish themes; these illustrate more powerfully the magic with which he is able to reduce and combine the elements in a natural scene until it is all ornament, ornament that arises from variety of surface, slimness of design and transparency of colour. On such works and upon others in which all conscious representation of nature has been abandoned but in which the interest of the surface variations, of gradings of colour, has been retained, the artist's celebrity might justly rely. But he has vainly consecrated much of his energy upon the production of large-scale works (sometimes in low relief) in which he has carried abstraction to the verge of a vacuum. The misconception underlying all abstract art is the belief that, in the context, the term abstraction can have more than a relative significance. Painting and sculpture must exist concretely if at all, and it is humanly impossible to invent forms or colours that have no counterpart in nature. Nicholson in his large designs, consisting of circles and right angles together or in isolation, impoverishes the potentialities of " abstract " art. It might, indeed, be argued that the square and the circle in these designs are not abstractions at all but merely imitations of geometrical abstractions. It is certain, at least, that the beauty of an abstract picture has no inevitable relation to its simplicity and the barrenness that Nicholson has cultivated has no pictorial interest. But it is still decorative in the dependent sense that simple shapes deliberately arranged have always been, and, as such alone, we may well feel that it should not be framed and hung but should be incorporated in some architectural scheme or used for other purposes of the applied arts. On the walls of a picture gallery the undue, the mute simplicity of these carefully conceived patterns would seem to proclaim in modern terms the Kantian fallacy that arabesque is the quintessence of artistic beauty.

IV. DEVELOPMENT OF THE NEO-ROMANTIC SPIRIT

The painting of Ben Nicholson is today a more isolated phenomenon than it was ten years ago. But the neo-romantic movement that has since that time established a pre-eminence among us remains sympathetic to an art whose limitations it has profitably experienced. This movement is a liberation from the emotional restraints of any purely plastic aim; but had not some such aim itself, at an earlier stage, offered freedom to the student from the traces of academic naturalism, the artistic imagination of today could not have claimed the liberties of expression which it now familiarly employs. If, in fact, there was any need to demonstrate the artificiality of descriptive labels, we might dwell upon the framework of abstraction within which neo-romance has shown itself. The term would be accurately applied not to the current idiom but to the admission of imaginative and emotional responses to life as the unending subject matter of art and to the relief with which the deadening limits have been recognised of any painting confined by formal or abstract preoccupations. This expansion of the artistic imagination was not confined to the painters, but enlarged and loosened the attitude of criticism.

Amid the throes of contemporary living, which hastened wherever they did not provoke the present imaginative reaction, the disturbed but ideal world of Blake and his disciples—to whom the aspirations of man seemed then as pressingly in need of salvage from his environment as they are today—has acquired a contemporary relevance. The religious but bucolic spirit of Samuel Palmer (1805–1881)—the most gifted of Blake's followers; the implicit summons in his pictures to mystical communion with nature and the everlasting upheavals of the seasons—exercises an infectious authority upon the present generation. Palmer's exalted vision has been discovered to be one of the most potent manifestations of the romantic genius in this country, though it remained exalted for the space of a few years only and the record of it is confined within a group of small pictures, mostly water-colours, drawings or engravings, revealing a fevered picture of what must be called a Saturnian age, whose pastures are also Christ's and whose swelling cornfields might be the scenes of Ruth's idyll. The powerful attraction that Blake's genius radiates today—the result not only of his desire for an unprejudiced liberation of the spiritual energies of humanity, but also of his gift for emphatic design and of the surrealist quality of his imagination—has led, by way of Palmer and his other disciple, Edward Calvert, the exponent also of a kind of biblical arcadia, to a revived interest in the whole, unequal achievement of the Romantic school. The imaginative world of the sublime and the terrible for which the artificial novels of Mary Shelley have provided the conventional symbol but whose real dramatic possibilities are most effectively realised in the violent imagery that is an instrument of her husband's poetry, now evokes a new interest, among critics of painting, as mirrored in the nightmare visions of Fuseli (1741–1825) or the Apocalyptic subjects, appropriately rendered on a gigantic scale, of John Martin (1789–1854). The extremes of fancy in which the idealism of the period expressed itself display a state of mind in which sanity might tremble; Thomas Wainwright (1794–1852), whose art, though for no reason to be deduced from the insignificance of his extant work, was admired by Blake, murdered his relations in law; and Richard Dadd (1817–1887), the subject of much recent research, died in Bethlehem Hospital, where he was confined for homicide. Interest in the art of the first half of the nineteenth century extends to the animal painter James Ward (1769–1859), whose curiously neurotic style was often the vehicle of extravagantly romantic subjects such as wild horses being pursued by wolves, or sanguinary conflicts between unlikely animals against a background of dramatic landscape. Even that somewhat later mutation of the Romantic school, Pre-Raphaelitism, which is perhaps closer to what is known as symbolist painting in France, now attracts an admiration for its sentimental intensity, so repugnant to the critical standards of advanced thought in the 'twenties. And the undisputed greatness of Constable and Turner is seen to reside not mainly in the prophetic impressionism of their vision, in the responsiveness of the one to the subtle changes of weather or of the other to the rarest effects of sunlight; it is now gratefully realised how much the beauty of Constable is the manifestation of a poetic attitude analogous to that of Wordsworth and how closely Turner's last and finest conceptions may be related to the cloudy empyrean evoked by Shelley. We even go so far as to prefer in Cézanne the artist who was passionately at the rigid but invaluable mercies of nature—the Cézanne of the water-colours and the final oil-paintings to the laborious architect of three-dimensional pattern whose structural peculiarities fathered, in this country, so many fruitless ambitions.

This most recent orientation of criticism may properly be considered as in part a reaction from the ideas of Roger Fry, a return to a freedom of attitude more easily acceptable to the temper of our culture, a freedom of attitude that might acquiesce in the inconsistencies of Ruskin but could not flourish under the system of Fry; but it also received strong support from the development on the continent of Surrealism, a movement whose deliberate exploitation of fantasies derived from the unconscious mind both warranted and prompted a revaluation of such artists as Palmer, Martin or Dadd. The Surrealist movement, however gross the miscalculation of its " primitive " efforts, has uncovered a field of imagery the potentialities of which remain to be fully exploited by artists, though it may be argued that they have already been stated, even in plastic or pictorial form, by propagandists. Chagall, Chirico and Picasso grow still more illustrious in our eyes as having given us, in advance, idealisations of the very raw material, arranged as on a dissecting table, by official Surrealism; the art of the surrealist, Max Ernst, which seems to reflect a consciousness of the utterly refractory quality of existence, of the balloon-like consistency of the least questionable of our values or motives, an art which has flowered into phantoms of the forces oppressing us from without or haunting us from within, is one of increasing contemporary relevance; and Klee's suffering puppets enfolded in veils of twittering colour, his evocation of the instantaneous poetry of childhood apprehensions, are the product of a surrealist alchemy whose processes, it may be guessed, will attract, in this country, a growing number of aspiring adepts. It must not be supposed that the neo-romantic tendency either of contemporary criticism or of contemporary painting is generally inspired by any exclusive worship of the native deities. For the last fifty years, at least, European art has evolved internationally; the present authority of Blake and Palmer has not so far been, and should not be allowed to become, the symbol of patriotic prejudice. Regionalism in art is only valuable when its fruits are either unconscious or, if not unconscious, at least genuinely temperamental.

Among the artists to be considered here under the vague heading of " neo-romanticism ", John Piper is, by temperament, most in tune with the national heritage. He is also a gifted critic and we may even accuse him, in this role, of a too persistent cultivation of the by-paths of our art history, of the minor, even the doubtful charms, for example, of neo-gothic urbanism. But as a painter, the character of his vision, with all its very English qualities, was not matured without the aid of foreign example and the native flavour of his work, at its best, is not the result of artificial intentions. As an exhibitor with the Seven and Five Group, his personality was in fee to the durance of abstract art, a discipline that he had been encouraged to acquire by contact with the work of Braque, Arp and Helion. He subsequently modified this manner, exhibiting in the middle 'thirties a series of collages, largely of coast scenes, and by about 1938 he had abandoned it for a romantic vision which, though still profiting from the lessons of abstraction, was distinctly descended from the English water-colourists of the late eighteenth and early nineteenth centuries, from the least trammelled productions of Alexander Cozens, Towne or Cotman and, less expectedly, from the highly-coloured topographical sketches of Edward Lear.[1] It is a vision that has revived the possibilities of the "picturesque" in the painting of landscape and architecture, possibilities which embrace the most dramatic of nature's effects and which Piper has developed with an unruffled skill and a vivid theatrical sentiment. Perhaps the most successful instance of the dramatic topography at which Piper excels is the series of water-colour drawings of Windsor Castle commissioned by the Queen in 1941. The charm of the subject must be sufficiently adventitious to the ordinary intelligent eye, but Piper's responsive interpretation has succeeded in imposing upon the useless battlements and turrets, with his dark skies and flashes of yellow light, an almost Spenserian magic. More recently, he completed a group of drawings of Renishaw Hall, in Derbyshire, full of a kind of British *morbidezza*, but in which the theatrical element was somewhat more crudely staged than in the Windsor series. As a painter of landscape, Piper has recently preferred the wilder aspects of the English scene, those to some extent in which James Ward also delighted, and his oils of Gordale Scar, a natural gorge, whose terrible aspect has been made known in the history of British painting by Ward's enormous canvas in the Tate Gallery, display a vigour and excitement that we do not always experience in looking at his paintings, in the same medium, of architecture, in which the wilfulness of strong colour contrasts is sometimes too apparent. Piper has also worked with natural success for the stage, designing scenery during the war for the ballets *The Quest* and *Façade* and subsequently for the recent production of Yeats' translation of *Oedipus*.

[1] 1812–1888. By profession a landscape painter, Lear is better known as the author of *Nonsense Verses*.

The influence of Samuel Palmer is evident in the earliest work of Graham Sutherland, who began as an engraver and as such first acquired a reputation. The unabashed but calculated licence of colour in his latest paintings may owe something to the same inspiration and to that of Blake. Sutherland is a painter of landscape, hitherto of mainly uninhabited landscape; but his mountains burning at sundown are the theatre of human passions and his woods are the womb of human impulses; and the grotesque bifurcation of the dead or dying tree-trunk which, in the first phase of his maturity, was the symbol of his predilection, seems to lay a disturbing stress on the insecurity of a faithless generation. He is the most powerful and the most frankly emotional of contemporary British painters. It was as a result of a visit, in 1936, to the noble but ominous scenery of Pembrokeshire in Wales, that he evolved his peculiar and eloquent conception of landscape forms. The earlier pictures of his maturity, in blacks, browns and reds, sounded a severe, almost a chiding note. Following upon a summer spent in a more verdant part of the country, he produced a group of canvases in rich, or at their weakest, in electric, greens in which the *sous-bois* motif, conceived mysteriously, predominated; the entrances to these woods are the threshold of secrets or, if the painter explores their hollows, it is to discover the death-throes of an oak or to surprise a conspiracy among the rocks. Such interpretations would be justified even if they were not explicitly invited by the titles of his paintings; the quality of his art is of a disturbing and suggestive kind that would gyrate in the imagination, if it was only to be encountered in curtains and carpets.

During the war years Sutherland took full advantage of his opportunity, as an official artist required, so to speak, to establish aesthetic contact with the reigning desolation, to broaden the appeal of his emotional vision of the human predicament. It was during these years that the human figure, in mines or in factories, began to play a distinct part in his work, and it seems certain that this part will develop, if the artist succeeds in achieving a personal domination of the technical difficulties that the figure presents. A lack of technical certainty is an intermittent defect of Sutherland's work, which, when it fails, declines towards an empty display of

Edward Burra, *Soldiers* (1942)

Henry Moore, *Draped Standing Figures* (1946)

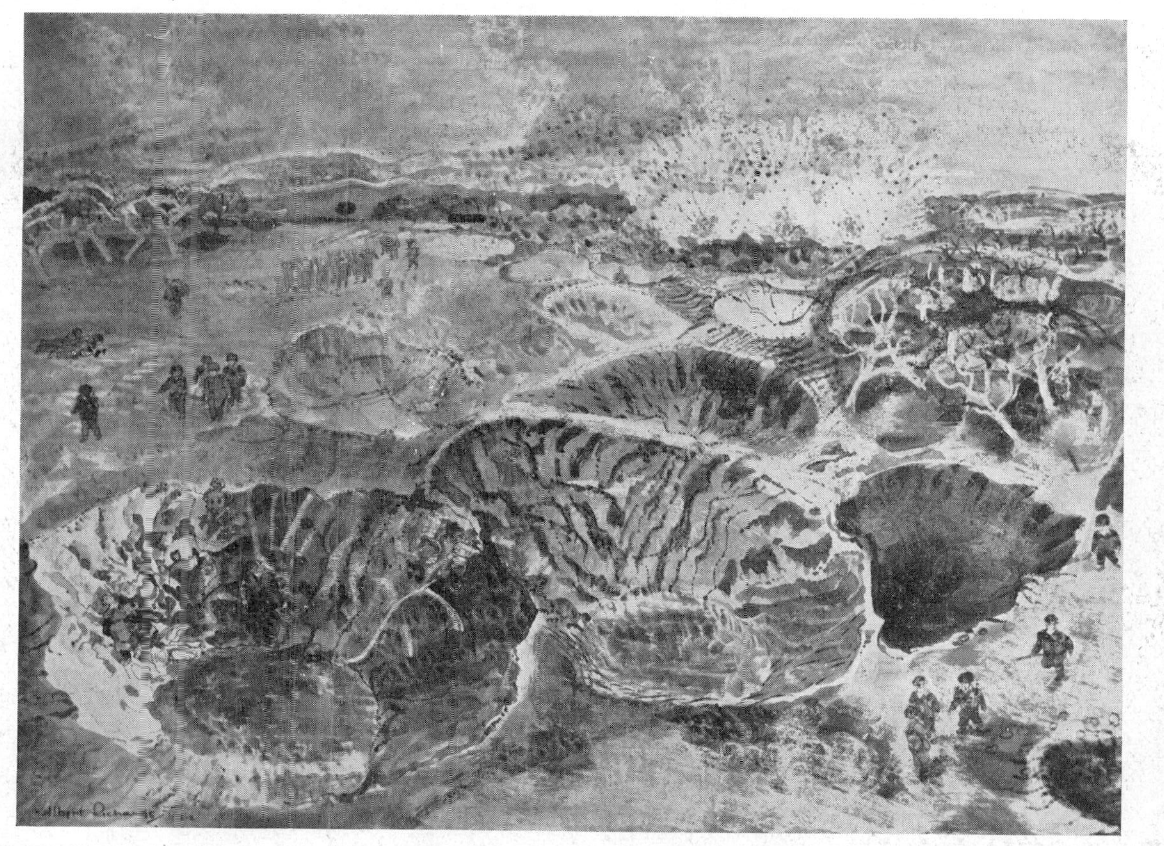

Albert Richards, *Withdrawing from the Battery* (1944)

Graham Sutherland, *Small Boulder* (1940)

virulent colour or to a crookedness of form that is mis-shapen without also being affecting. There is no lack of charity in calling attention to this defect in an artist for whom, it is clear, the future holds so many possibilities in store; since the war, Sutherland has been seen to be enlarging the range of his imagery; he has made the surrealist bull, already an almost accepted symbol, live for his special purposes; and his latest exhibited pictures are jagged structures, founded upon the crown of thorns and set against a background of madonna-like blue that he has not used before.

Henry Moore is properly a sculptor, but there is impressive proof of a painter's talent in his regular output of coloured drawings, many of them conceived, paradoxically enough, as projects for sculpture and nearly all of them valued for their vivid pictorial qualities. Moore has been an abstract sculptor and has exhibited with the Surrealists both in England and abroad. The surrealist element in his imagination has remained, but during the war his study of air-raid shelterers and, later, his commissions to carve a Virgin and Child for St. Mary's Church, Northampton, and a statue representing the Family (of which only maquettes are extant) for Impington College, developed his vision in a less arbitrary direction which, while it lasts, may aptly be described as neo-romantic. These works, though less so than the reclining figures of the period preceding the war, still convey the impression of a kind of anthropomorphic still-life, at once profoundly human in conception and suggesting, in their forms, sub-human organisms; but their anatomy is less boldly adulterated, and though this has involved no loss of force in any of the preliminary sketches, the finished group of the Virgin and Child appears to have suffered, perhaps inevitably in the circumstances, from a softening of the original idea. In the absence of any regular patronage of sculpture, Moore's art may be more widely known through his drawings. Some of the best of these date from shortly before the war. The figures they depict, standing, seated or reclining in hieratic attitudes, secreting within themselves the clue to their apparently preordained immobility, are likely more and more to impose their example upon younger painters who will sympathise with the impassive resignation of these occasionally mutilated beings among the irrelevant harmonies of shifting colour which encompass them. The depths and transparencies of Moore's colour, produced, usually, by the most deft handling of a combination of gouache, water-colour and greasy chalk, are the source of the instantaneous attraction of his pictures. As a sculptor whose first concern is with the expression of form, he has achieved the feat of animating his shapes, in themselves austere if not impassive, with a subtle emotional complexion, of presenting them in an atmosphere almost of passion that is the result of an instinctive colour sense operating not only dramatically but also as an organ of taste, so that his drawings provide at first sight, before we have penetrated their details, a sensuous stimulus. They have an assurance of execution, and an impartiality—almost priestly because it is not careless—in the human sympathies they express.

It has become a naturally accepted convention to link the names of John Piper, Graham Sutherland and Henry Moore as the chief protagonists of the contemporary school, especially in so far as British painting now exhibits neo-romantic tendencies. But any account of these tendencies must consider the more isolated and less influential work of Edward Burra, who acquired a reputation in the 'twenties as a painter of sardonic genre, of scenes from the world of the cheaper night-clubs, of dubious bars and *escales*. In the late 'thirties, moved by the tragedy of the Spanish Civil War, he acquired a more bitter, less satiric view of the character of the age, which the outbreak of the World War subsequently confirmed. The large, livid water-colours that were the outcome of this deeper reaction, with their florid emphasis—too little distilled by art—on the spectacle of strife and desolation, have nevertheless a great force of presentation which compels a surprised attention. Owing more to inspired gleanings from the illustrated press of the world than to the example of any more recognised artistic influence, they are carried out in a naturalistic manner which may (though it is a possibility that is stated with some temerity) derive something of its flavour from Salvador Dali; it is one that is effective by direct statement, though it is mostly an allegory that is stated. In Burra's evocations of the Spanish war, tanks and halberdiers appear side by side, figures in doublets are protected by tin helmets, poetic anachronisms that wrap up the tragedy in a cloak of historical splendour. *Soldiers*, the most powerful of his recent pictures, is one of his least palatable. Its frieze of uncomfortable figures, helmeted, grotesquely masked—as it might be, by gas-masks—and swathed in the restrictive folds of some indistinguishable battle-dress, is a vehement comment upon contemporary army life. Distressing as such painting may be, by the boldness of its colour and the crude vigour of its drawing, as much as by its unequivocal purport, it is not difficult to acknowledge its value as an imaginative expression, too rough and overwrought, of the violence of the times.

V. THE WORK OF THE WAR ARTISTS ADVISORY COMMITTEE

On the outbreak of war, the inevitable danger, that would otherwise have followed the overriding necessities of conscription, of a total interruption of the development of artistic talent, was met by the Government through the establishment of the War Artists Advisory Committee under the Ministry of Information. This Committee ensured the maintenance in the exercise of their vocation of all those artists whom they considered capable of giving aesthetic expression to the tragedies, the endeavours or the nausea that were begotten by the conflict or who could, in the Committee's opinion, record, in artistic terms, its scenes and events. Artists were either commissioned for the duration of the war or were employed on a limited number of pictures covering a specific subject. It was open to any artist to submit a picture for acquisition by the Committee. All the works commissioned or acquired are the property of the nation; they were exhibited throughout the war at the National Gallery, and are now to be distributed to museums throughout the country and to other public or to service institutions. This imaginative and generous scheme was the effective instrument of the continuity of British painting during the six years of war; its results were catholic and no purposes of art criticism would be served by excusing or condemning the failures that such a project was bound, inadvertently or mistakenly, to patronise. But its successes were marked.

Under its auspices, the water-colour art of the late Eric Ravilious developed a final vividness in his unimpassioned recordings of the naval war. Ravilious had, in peace-time, been largely active as an engraver, book illustrator and designer for the applied arts. His work for the War Artists Committee continued to display the linear grace and faint, clean colour for which his water-colours were already known. But his gift for formalisation was sharpened by the requirements of accurate observation and his ships and sea-planes were stylised into decorative units while retaining their specific character. He succeeded in preserving his precise, designer's personality even in the record of naval actions; his war art is a refreshing, acutely seen vision, in tabloid form, of the smooth performance and neat machinery that we associate with naval activities.

Edward Bawden, a polished water-colourist, whose name has often been coupled with that of Ravilious, practises a more sensitive art and, as a war artist, his talent has been more obviously enlarged. Without revealing in his pictures any deep response to the enormity of events, he evolved a lyrical, legendary perception of the skies and domes of the Middle East that provided a nervous contrast with the practical military activities that proceeded in their midst. A vaguely satirical attitude to life had inspired his painting before the war; and he expressed the romance of Cairo, Addis Ababa and Gallabat the better, perhaps, because it was so ill attuned to the spectacle of mechanised warfare.

The artistic value of many of the works commissioned by the Committee may increase when time has enabled us to judge it in conjunction with their historical interest. But it was lawful and inevitable that the scheme should have triumphed through those works in which destruction and tragedy, the salient elements of modern war—unmitigable by any other of its aspects—were most earnestly interpreted. Graham Sutherland's shattered streets materially beautified by devastation and by the lurid but poetic colours with which they were invested in his eyes, Henry Moore's underground shelterers, their exhausted forms locked together in

pressionist ideal. But the ardour of the *rapin* proved powerless to reanimate it; the efforts of the group, with few exceptions, have mainly served to flatter the timid critic or to provide the contemporary note in the collections of cautious connoisseurs. It is possible that the causes of this revival are to be sought in the prestige of Sickert and more particularly in a half political ambition to cultivate the element of conscious social comment that distinguished Sickert's impressionism from that of most of his contemporaries; but the group, celebrated for a moment as the Euston Road School, has failed to survive, and many of its adherents are drifting into the orbit of the "official" Royal Academy where the *pleinairisme* that flourished at the New English Art Club in the eighties of the last century is now generally accepted. The Euston Road School seems never to have had any collective critical significance; that, for a fleeting period culminating in an exhibition at Oxford in 1941, it promised to develop a theoretic cohesion, if not a policy, was due to the intellectual ardour of one of its members, the late Graham Bell, whose acute qualities of mind may have dulled in him any instinctive appreciation of the elegant sensuousness of his own artistic gift. His opinions on social questions led others, temporarily, to choose their subjects from among the least interesting aspects of urban life with the object of establishing a socialist, if not a proletarian realism in painting. But the political moment passed; the group disintegrated, and its acknowledged leader and most talented member, Victor Pasmore, was left, since his individuality did not require the support of association, in isolation. Pasmore is not an Impressionist, but his art is exposed to the unflattering interpretation that he is a painter whose chief sanction is in that school. He began as an Impressionist and the dominating influence upon his early work was Sickert's. He appears now, however, as a Whistlerian, even an Oriental, landscape painter, capable, from a starting point in nature, of slowly producing, by a process of blending, eliminating, regrouping and re-colouring, a self-sufficient object of the subtlest kind of luxury. The gloomy, urban realities that inspired Sickert had no lasting message for him; if it should be said that he should find the pretext of his compositions in any particular of nature, then the complexities of rime, the waving of

an oppressive half-light, and Paul Nash's fabulous depictions of t wreckage of the aeroplanes, overshadow any pictorial record of t fortitude with which the struggle was conducted or the disaste endured. It has been truthfully pointed out how the specialise qualities of Moore and Sutherland were made vivid to a large publi when they were seen to be the sign of emotions that had bee generally experienced.

Although the War Artists Committee gathered within its fold an important proportion of existing talent, it could not, in the circumstances of the war, make many new discoveries. It is evidence of the wisdom of its direction that it was empowered to secure the release from military service of any artist that it might discover and consider capable of making a positive contribution to its activities. The late Albert Richards, who was killed in 1945 at the age of twenty-six, was the only case of the kind. The limited number of his works that were acquired show a degree of precocious achievement rather than the promise of some undeveloped maturity. They embody features of the art of Moore, Sutherland and Piper but have a personal, curious gaiety of colour that spreads over his pictures animating every part so that they produce a kind of vernal glitter in which their subjects, mainly incidents in the land war, are effaced. The trees, the ground, the paraphernalia of camouflage, even the lurking soldier, are merged together in a natural scene that may be understood to be a scene of dramatic happenings only through the fevered but garden brightness of the colour. His discovery was rewarding, and the public acquisition of what were probably his best pictures is at least an adequate memorial of the tragedy of his early death.

VI. THE RISING GENERATION

The two most venerable exponents of British Impressionism, Walter Sickert (1860–1942) and Philip Wilson Steer (1860–1942), died during the war. The former had, towards the close of the 'thirties, to some natural extent actively countenanced the revival among a group of young painters of the already threadbare Im-

spring grasses and other such tenuous but vivid phenomena might be expected to secrete for him the potentialities that would be most useful to his imagination. The snow scenes painted at the end of the war from his studio on the Chiswick reach of the Thames are full of diaphanous texture and capricious lines that subsist in a Chinese independence of natural appearances; it is an independence conceived within the framework of the Impressionist convention, but it is the essence of Pasmore's value and saves him from the academism into which many of his former colleagues have subsided. Of these, the youngest, Lawrence Gowing, is deservedly respected for the technical strength and conscientious energy with which he pursues what is fundamentally an Impressionist ideal. The austere variation upon the Impressionist manner announced in the earlier work of William Coldstream has not, apparently, been so far further developed.

Victor Pasmore is a mature artist, but more than one of his original fellow-travellers on the Euston Road are young workers, and the momentary modernity that the group appeared to have bestowed upon the familiar character of British Impressionism may explain the attraction that this old mode of expression continues to exercise upon numbers of the younger generation. Their careers prosper; but their work provides no key to the possible future of British painting. Indeed, in the present circumstances, we can make no confident assertion about the prospects of the contemporary school. Since, for six years, it would have been idle in the young to consider, practically, the possibilities of vocation, we are still ignorant of the extent and quality of the artistic faculties with which they may be endowed. Talent, under the exactions of universal conscription for war, does not visibly germinate. That genius necessarily expresses itself would in peace-time be a controversial claim, for we cannot know in how many cases it is made mute and inglorious by some defect of will or pressure of normal events; it is doubly improbable that it should have forced a way under the pressure of the abnormal situation in which everyone still exists. Yet, though the strength of the visions which may have been gathering or waning in elect but frustrated minds is unknown to us, we may try to envisage the broad spiritual area in which the artistic imagination is likely to assume exterior shape and colour. Artistic tendencies are independent, as personalities cannot be, of social and political upheavals and may even appear to presage their character, progressing, as history has shown them to do so far, with a dynastic sweep which, if only to the most abstracted scrutiny, may seem more fateful than the fugitive disruptions of past wars. The character of British painting as illustrated in the few artists sufficiently young and stimulating to claim consideration as the exponents of future developments is one with which the stresses of modern life are likely to be in increasing accord; it bears within it the consciousness that hopes of spiritual safety are perilous; it is fanciful, but its fancies have an anarchistic or derisive flavour; its imagination plays upon aspirations that may be subconsciously pursued but never consciously satisfied; it appears, in the company of Moore and Sutherland, to look upon nature as evading the repressive machinations of man and upon man himself as the victim as much of his own nature as of society. It is upon those younger artists who are in sympathy with the achievement of Moore and Sutherland that we must found any forecast of future directions. They are artists who would not feel secure in the repetition of what has been repeated, who reserve the freedom to stumble and appear ridiculous; their work may give less satisfaction to many honest minds than the impressionistic products of those whose fervour has been tempered by a prudence cautioning them to neglect the changes of the last forty years; they may borrow from sources that have not received the sanction of tradition and their adaptation of the forms and symbols is sometimes undisguised and even graceless. The inspiration of Palmer sustains, and Sutherland's influence sporadically weakens, the precocious vision of John Craxton; the bursting, moonlit growths of nature, as seen by Palmer's disturbed eye, have reappeared with scant modification in the art of John Minton; Max Ernst's uneasy foliations, his immutable stellar circles, have been used by Ceri Richards. The very amateur pictures of Lucien Freud have a distinctly idiosyncratic nature, though the grotesque *naïveté* of his vagrant humour seems indebted to the almost philosophical infantilism of some of Klee's pictures. The prestige of Moore, Sutherland and Piper is most plainly acknowledged

Henry Moore, *Seated Figure and Pointed Forms* (1940)

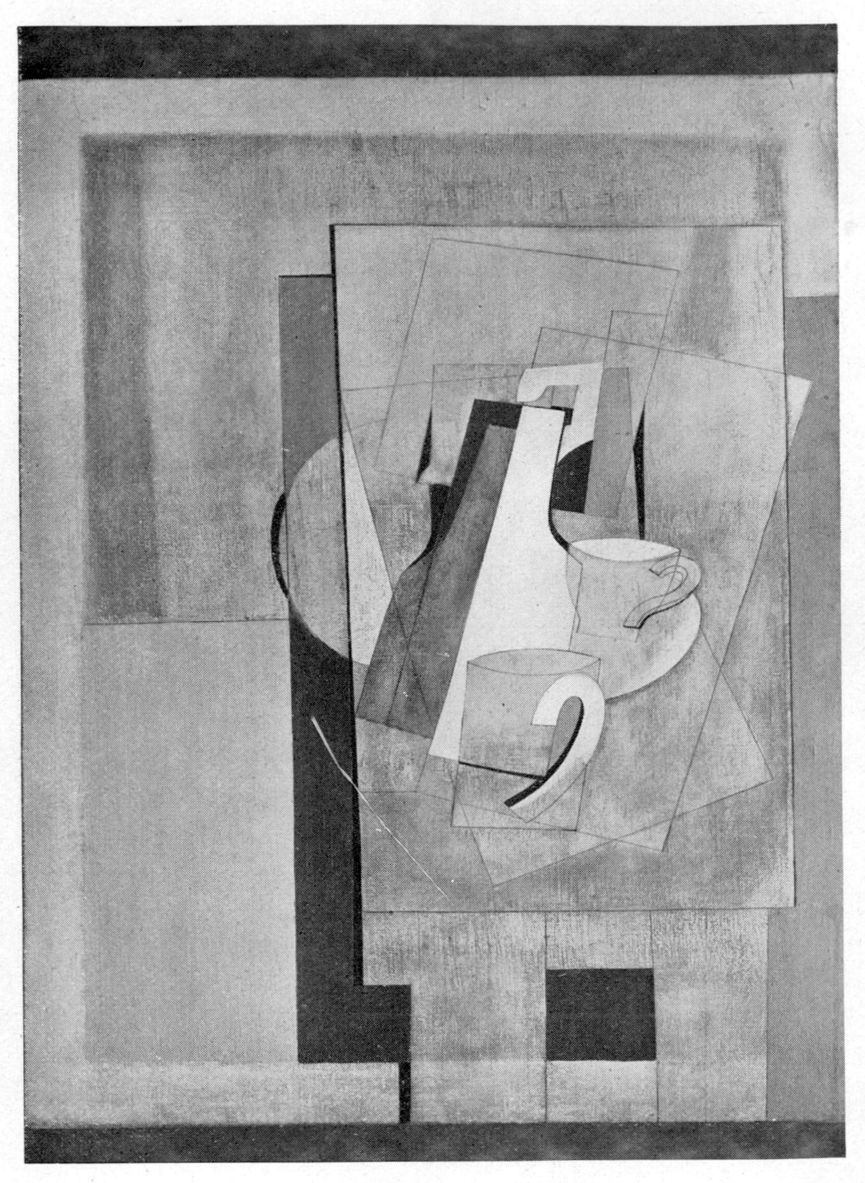

Ben Nicholson, *Still Life*, 1945

Stanley Spencer, *Christ in the Wilderness—The Scorpions* (1939)

Victor Pasmore, *Everlasting Flowers* (1941)

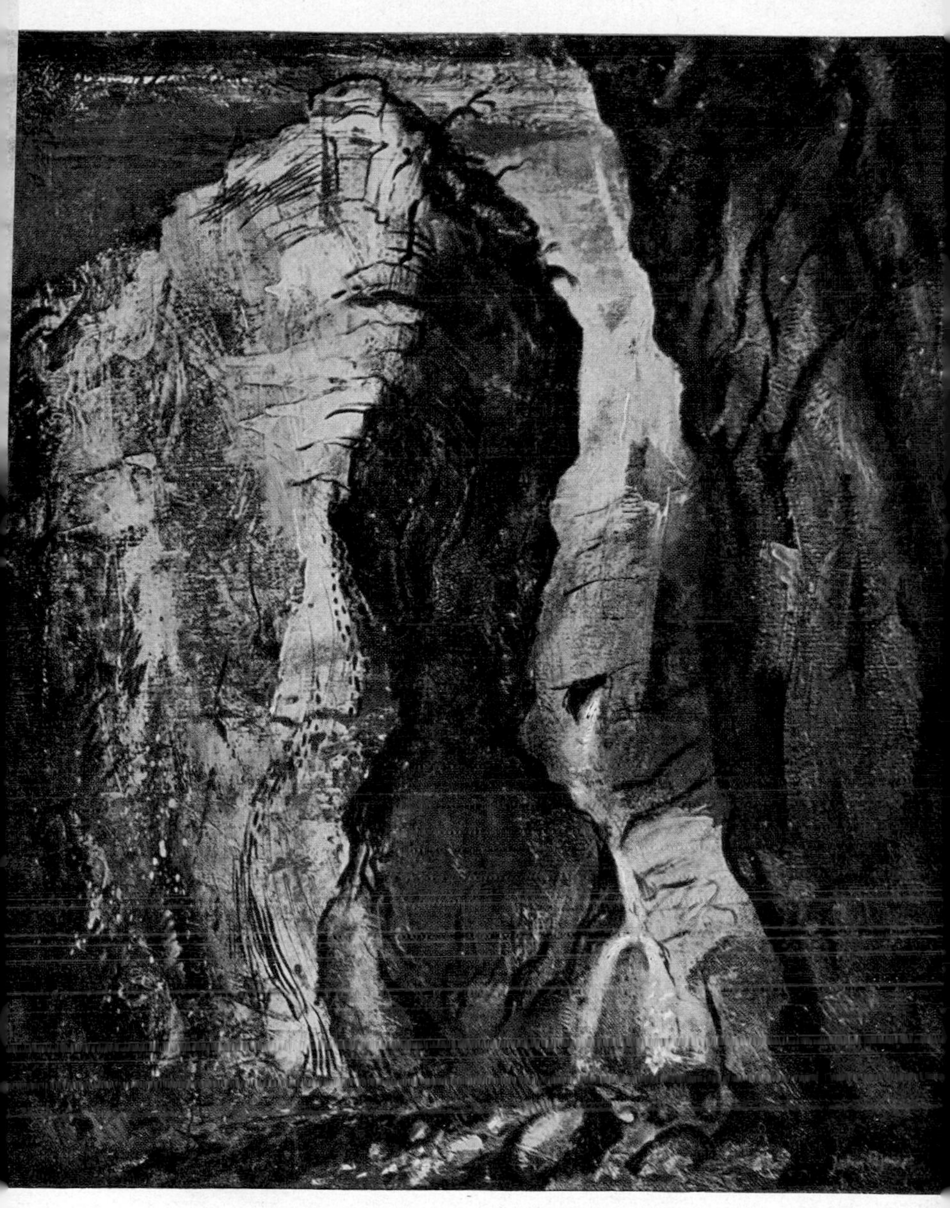

John Piper, *Gordale Scar* (1943)

Ceri Richards, *Blossoms*

Frances Hodgkins, *Wings Over Water*

John Craxton, *Alderholt Mill, Dorset* (1944)

by the mannerism of Keith Vaughan, a tribute that conciliates criticism as much by its skill as its candour. The art of Francis Bacon is also in apparent debt to that of Sutherland; his large ferocious studies (recently exhibited) for a Crucifixion bear a close temperamental relation to Sutherland's less virulent (and probably antecedent) conception of thorn structures. And the younger group of Glasgow painters, of whom the most prominent are Robert Colquhoun and Ian MacBryde, owe something to the example of surrealistic influences from Europe.

It is easy to demonstrate these debts; they are noted here not as a ground of disparagement but with the purpose of recognising the wisdom which incurred them. While it is impossible to foresee whether the combination of artistic influences now at work in Great Britain will bring forth any show of genius, whether, for example, the art of Henry Moore will be succeeded by any manifestation at a comparable imaginative level, it seems certain that, short of drastic State direction, provided, that is to say, that the art of painting remains, as it now is, an esoteric one, its development in this country will pursue the tendencies being adopted by the younger imaginative painters. There is at present no likelihood of the alternative of a reaction towards abstraction, or, as it would now be called, non-figurative painting. We may feel at this moment the sympathetic relationship with human desires and uncertainties to which the imaginative art of the younger generation aspires. It is not an art that could produce an object of "virtu", a collector's piece, in its own day; but, like other valid expressions of European culture, it seeks to associate the beauty at which it aims with the less accessible channels of individual existences.

LONDON, 1945

BIOGRAPHICAL NOTES ON THE CONTEMPORARY ARTISTS REFERRED TO IN THE TEXT

* denotes that the work of the painter is represented in the Tate Gallery, the national collection of contemporary art

FRANCIS BACON. b. 1910. Largely self-taught.

EDWARD BAWDEN.* b. 1903. Water-colour painter. Has also executed illustrations for fine books and theatrical décors. Born at Braintree, Essex. Studied at the Cambridge School of Art and at the Royal College of Art (London). Assistant Professor in the School of Design at the Royal College of Art. As an official war artist, worked chiefly in the Middle East.

GRAHAM BELL.* 1910–1943. Painter of portraits and landscapes. Born in the Transvaal, S. Africa. Killed in an aircraft accident while training as an R.A.F. navigator.

EDWARD BURRA.* b. 1905. Water-colour painter. Born in London. Studied at the Chelsea School of Art (London). Travelled in the U.S.A. and Europe. Has exhibited with the English Surrealists.

WILLIAM COLDSTREAM.* b. 1908. Painter mainly of portraits. Born at Belford, Northumberland. Studied at the Slade School, London. Worked for the Post Office Film Unit, 1934–1937.

ROBERT COLQUHOUN. b. 1914. Studied at the Glasgow School of Art and subsequently, with the aid of a travelling scholarship, in France and Italy.

JOHN CRAXTON. b. 1920. Studied at the Goldsmiths' College and the Westminster School of Art.

LUCIEN FREUD. b. 1922. Studied sculpture at the London County Council School of Arts and Crafts, also worked at the East Anglia School of Painting and Drawing; but has been mainly self-taught.

LAWRENCE GOWING.* b. 1918. Painter of landscapes, portraits and still-life. Born at Stoke Newington.

DUNCAN GRANT.* b. 1885. Painter chiefly of landscape, still-life and portraits. Designer for textiles, pottery and the theatre. Born at Rothiemurchus, Inverness-shire (Scotland). Studied at the Westminster and Slade Schools (London) and in Italy and Paris.

IVON HITCHENS.* b. 1893. Painter chiefly of landscape and still-life. Born in London. Studied at the St. John's Wood School of Art (London) and at the Royal Academy Schools (London). Member of the Seven and Five Group.

FRANCES HODGKINS.* 1870–1947. Painter chiefly of landscape and still-life. Born in New Zealand. Attended no art schools. Came to Europe, 1900. Settled in Paris, 1902, where she taught at the Académie Colarossi. Painted in Cornwall, 1914–1919. Member of the Seven and Five Group.

DAVID JONES.* b. 1895. Painter, chiefly in water-colour, and engraver of animal, landscape and romantic subjects. Born at Brockley, Kent, of Welsh descent. Studied at the Camberwell and Westminster Art Schools (London). Won the Hawthornden Prize for literature (1938) with *In Parenthesis*, a poetic account of his experiences in the first World War. Member of the Seven and Five Group.

IAN MACBRYDE. b. 1913. Studied at the Glasgow School of Art and subsequently, with the aid of a travelling scholarship, in France and Italy.

JOHN MINTON. b. 1918. Studied at the St. John's Wood Art School, London. Teacher at the Camberwell Art School, London.

HENRY MOORE.* b. 1898. Sculptor. Born at Castleford, Yorkshire. Studied at the Leeds School of Art, and at the Royal College of Art (London) where he won a travelling scholarship which took him to France and Italy. Member of the Seven and Five Group. Has exhibited with the Surrealists in England and abroad. Official war artist.

PAUL NASH.* 1893–1946. Painter of landscape, book illustrator and designer for applied art. Born at Dymchurch, Kent. Studied at the Slade School (London). Official artist both in the war of 1914–1918 and in the recent war. Has exhibited with the Surrealists.

BEN NICHOLSON.* b. 1894. Abstract painter. Born at Denham, Buckinghamshire, the son of the painter Sir William Nicholson. Studied at the Slade School (London), at Tours, Milan and at Pasadena (U.S.A.). Member of the association Abstraction-Création (Paris), 1933–1934, and of the Seven and Five Group.

VICTOR PASMORE.* b. 1900. Painter chiefly of landscape, portraits and still-life. Born at Chelsham, Surrey. Attended no art schools. Worked in the Civil Service, 1927–1937.

JOHN PIPER.* b. 1903. Painter of architecture and landscape and writer on artistic subjects. Born at Epsom, Surrey. Studied at the Richmond and Slade Schools (London) and at the Royal College of Art (London). Official war artist.

ERIC RAVILIOUS.* 1903–1942. Water-colour painter, engraver and decorator. Born in London. Studied at the Eastbourne School of Art, and at the Royal College of Art (London) where he became instructor in drawing. Official war artist. Lost his life, while attached to the Royal Air Force, in an accident on a flight from Iceland.

ALBERT RICHARDS.* 1919–1945. Painter chiefly in water-colour. Studied at the Wallasey School of Art and at the Royal College of Art (London). Official war artist (transferred from the army). Killed in 1945.

CERI RICHARDS.* b. 1903. Painter of Surrealist subjects. Born at Swansea, Glamorganshire (Wales). Studied at the Swansea School of Art and at the Royal College of Art (London).

MATTHEW SMITH.* b. 1879. Painter of still-life, landscape and figures. Born at Halifax, Yorkshire. Studied at the Manchester School of Art and at the Slade School (London). Visited Paris, 1910. Until 1939, lived alternately in France and England.

STANLEY SPENCER.* b. 1892. Painter of imaginative and religious subjects, of landscape and occasional portraits. Born at Cookham, Berkshire. Studied at the Slade School (London). Travelled in Italy, Yugoslavia and Switzerland. Decorated with wall paintings the Chapel at Burghclere, Berkshire, 1926–1934. Official war artist.

GRAHAM SUTHERLAND.* b. 1903. Painter of imaginative subjects. Born in London. Studied at the Goldsmiths' School of Art (London). Practised mainly as engraver and illustrator until the early 'thirties. Official war artist.

KEITH VAUGHAN. b. 1917. Began his career as a commercial artist in the Unilever Studios. Now a teacher at the Camberwell Art School, London.

ETHEL WALKER.* b. 1877. Painter of portraits, flower-pieces, sea-pieces and decorative compositions. Born in Edinburgh. Studied at the Westminster and Slade Schools (London). Attended evening classes under Walter Sickert.

47